A TREASURY *of* PRAISE

ENJOYING GOD ANEW

RUTH MYERS
with WARREN MYERS

MULTNOMAH
BOOKS

A TREASURY OF PRAISE
PUBLISHED BY MULTNOMAH BOOKS
12265 Oracle Boulevard, Suite 200
Colorado Springs, Colorado 80921
A division of Random House Inc.

All Scripture quotations, unless otherwise indicated, are taken from the New American Standard Bible®. © Copyright The Lockman Foundation 1960, 1962, 1963, 1968, 1971, 1973, 1975, 1977, 1995. Used by permission. (www.Lockman.org). Scripture quotations marked (AMP) are taken from The Amplified® Bible. Copyright © 1954, 1958, 1962, 1964, 1965, 1987 by The Lockman Foundation. Used by permission. (www.Lockman.org). Scripture quotations marked (ESV) are taken from The Holy Bible, English Standard Version, copyright © 2001 by Crossway Bibles, a division of Good News Publishers. Used by permission. All rights reserved. Scripture quotations marked (KJV) are taken from the King James Version. Scripture quotations marked (Laubach) are taken from *The Inspired Letters in Clearest English* by Frank C. Laubach. Copyright © 1956 by Thomas Nelson Inc. Scripture quotations marked (MSG) are taken from The Message by Eugene H. Peterson. Copyright © 1993, 1994, 1995, 1996, 2000, 2001, 2002. Used by permission of NavPress Publishing Group. All rights reserved. Scripture quotations marked (MLB) are taken from The Modern Language Bible: The Berkeley Version in Modern English, Revised Edition, copyright © 1945, 1959, 1969 by Hendrickson Publishers Inc. Used by permission. Scripture quotations marked (Moffatt) are taken from The Bible: James Moffatt Translation by James A. R. Moffatt. Copyright © 1954 by James A. R. Moffatt. Harper Collins Inc. and Hodder and Stoughton Ltd. Scripture quotations marked (NCV) are taken from the New Century Version®. Copyright © 1987, 1988, 1991 by Thomas Nelson Inc. Used by permission. All rights reserved. Scripture quotations marked (NIV) are taken from the Holy Bible, New International Version®. NIV®. Copyright © 1973, 1978, 1984 by International Bible Society. Used by permission of Zondervan Publishing House. All rights reserved. Scripture quotations marked (NKJV) are taken from the New King James Version®. Copyright © 1982 by Thomas Nelson Inc. Used by permission. All rights reserved. Scripture quotations marked (NLT) are taken from the Holy Bible, New Living Translation, copyright © 1996. Used by permission of Tyndale House Publishers Inc., Wheaton, Illinois 60189. All rights reserved. Scripture quotations marked (Phillips) are taken from The New Testament in Modern English, Revised Edition © 1972 by J. B. Phillips. Copyright renewed © 1986, 1988 by Vera M. Phillips. Scripture quotations marked (RSV) are taken from the Revised Standard Version of the Bible, copyright © 1952, 1971 by the Division of Christian Education of the National Council of the Churches of Christ in the USA. Used by permission. All rights reserved. Scripture quotations marked (TLB) are taken from The Living Bible, copyright © 1971. Used by permission of Tyndale House Publishers Inc., Wheaton, Illinois 60189. All rights reserved. Scripture quotations marked (Weymouth) are taken from The New Testament in Modern Speech © 1903, 1904, 1909, 1912, translated by Richard Francis Weymouth; edited and revised by Ernest Hampden-Cook. Scripture quotations marked (Williams) are taken from The New Testament: A Translation in the Language of the People by Charles B. Williams, copyright © 1937 Moody Bible Institute. Used by permission.

This book incorporates content originally included in: *31 Days of Praise* © 1994 by Warren and Ruth Myers; *31 Days of Power* © 2003 by Ruth Myers; *ChristLife* © 2005 by Ruth Myers

ISBN 978-1-59052-961-4

MULTNOMAH is a trademark of Multnomah Books, and is registered in the U.S. Patent and Trademark Office. The colophon is a trademark of Multnomah Books.

Printed in the United States of America
2007—First Edition

10 9 8 7 6 5 4 3 2 1

Contents

An Invitation to Praise

*I*f you're just beginning to praise and worship, you're on the threshold of a great adventure. You'll find that your gracious, mighty, and majestic God is delightful beyond imagining. You'll discover what a high privilege it is to praise Him! And whether you're a beginner or someone who has long understood the benefits of praise, you'll find that the more you glorify the Lord, the more He will refresh you and deepen your experience of Him.

Woven into this book you'll find truths about God that affirm A. W. Tozer's words: "The man who has God as his treasure has all things in one, and he has it purely, legitimately, and forever."

Our Goal: A Lifestyle of Praise

The days of praise in this book have been designed to help you praise and give thanks both in your times of blessing and in your times of trial. These praise pages will expand your praise life and help you develop the practice of "giving thanks always for all things" (Ephesians 5:20, NKJV). They will help you cultivate a lifestyle of praise.

But before you begin, let's take a look at what praise is and why it's so important—why it's more than a pleasant pastime.

In the Bible, praise is closely linked with worship and thanksgiving. Through all three we honor and enjoy God. It helps me to think of worship as a beautiful crown adorned with two brilliant jewels. One jewel is praise; the other, thanksgiving.

Worship

Worship is our greatest privilege, the highest thing we can do.

In genuine spiritual worship, we bow before the Most High God, the most merciful and reliable and winsome of all beings, and we crown Him as Lord of all that we are. We consent to His gracious, transforming work; we agree that He can work in us so that we'll be willing and able to do His will. In other words, we choose to let Him be God in our lives.

Worship includes yielding to God as our Lord and Master. We see this in Romans 12:1, where God asks us to offer Him our bodies, our lives, our entire person. This, He says, is true worship.

Praise

Praise includes adoring God and admiring Him for who He is and what He does.

Praise can be quiet and meditative. But it can also be celebrating and exulting in the Lord's majesty and splendor, His sovereignty, His limitless power, and His bountiful love—which we do not in the least deserve. In praise we extol our wonderful God; we exalt and magnify Him.

Praise includes speaking highly of God to other people as well as directly to Him.

Thanksgiving

Thanksgiving is appreciating God and letting Him know how grateful we are for His mighty works and the blessings He bestows on us.

In thanksgiving we express gratitude to the Lord for His love and goodness to us and to others, for His constant acts of care, and for His gifts, including the spiritual blessings He has lavished upon us.

So mounted in the crown of worship—the basic act of offering God our lives, of honoring Him as God—are the jewels of praise and thanksgiving, jewels that radiate the glory of God, to His delight and ours.

All three of these—worship, praise, and thanksgiving—overlap as we glorify and enjoy God. Sometimes we do this in speaking, sometimes in singing, sometimes in silent reverence.

It's fine if we blend worship, praise, and thanksgiving any way we like. God isn't in the least concerned if we say "Thank You" when "I praise You" or "I worship You" might be more appropriate. And it doesn't matter whether our words are stumbling or eloquent. God looks on the heart; He's searching for people who simply want to honor Him.

How Can We Praise God and Be Thankful in Every Situation?

A life of praise may appeal to you. But what does it involve? You may be puzzled about what it means to praise *continually* and give thanks always, in every situation. Won't this lead to denying your true feelings? Does it mean that when you stub your toe or hit your thumb with a hammer, your spontaneous response must be "Thank You, Lord"? Isn't it dishonest to give thanks if you don't feel thankful?

Several things have helped settle these questions for me.

It's Based on More Than Feelings

One is that the Bible doesn't command us to feel thankful in every situation. It doesn't command us to manufacture positive feelings. Instead, it commands us to give thanks (1 Thessalonians 5:18). As Dr. John G. Mitchell, cofounder of Multnomah School of the Bible, put it: "To give thanks when you don't feel like it is not hypocrisy; it's obedience."

This does not mean you should deny your negative thoughts and feelings and attitudes, sweeping them under some inner emotional rug. It doesn't mean you should repress them into some deep cavern where, again and again, they can sneak back into your thoughts, press you into unwise choices, and filter past your defenses to pollute the emotional atmosphere around you.

Notice that David and the other psalmists were honest about their feelings, facing them and telling God about them. They knew how to pour out their heart before Him (Psalm 62:8). Often they praised God first and then expressed their disturbed emotions, their perplexities, even their complaints. After this they went on to praise God again, despite their struggles. They did not deny their feelings or simply ignore them. Nor did they wallow in them until they'd all but drowned. And it doesn't seem that they postponed their praise until they had worked through their emotions and felt better. Instead, they mingled an honest pouring-out of their feelings with sincere, God-honoring praise.

Take, for example, Psalm 42. The psalmist composed this song in a time of exile and oppression, when he felt deeply disturbed and downcast. People were saying, "Where is your God—why doesn't He do something for you if He's the true and living God?" The psalmist told God how troubled his heart was. But even as he did so, he honored God, speaking of Him as "the living God…my God…the God of my life…God my rock…the help of my countenance." His every reference to God showed his desire to exalt and glorify Him. And he assured his soul that the time would come when he could once again join the festal worship in the house of God and praise the Lord for deliverance. Psalm 43, written in a similar situation, likewise honors God in very special ways: "O God…the God of my strength…God my exceeding joy…my God."

What happens when we follow the example of the psalmists—when we express our impressions and feelings yet choose to keep praising in spite of how things seem to us? I find that sooner or later (often sooner) the Lord releases me from being a slave to my distressing emotions. He unties the tight knots within me and settles my feelings, though He may not answer my questions about how He's handling my affairs. And when at times praise does not quickly bring inner freedom and joy, I can say, "Lord, I can't praise You in the same way I did last week (or last year). I can't seem to respond to You with the same sense of delight and celebration. But I do choose to lift You high, praising You for what You are and what You mean to me."

Life—and praise—isn't always a feast of pure, simple gladness. Don't you find that in many situations you can experience both pleasant and unpleasant emotions? Like Paul, you can be "sorrowful yet always rejoicing" (2 Corinthians 6:10). You can groan and suffer in this fallen world, yet you can learn to rejoice. You can learn to triumph in your hope, in your tribulations and the good things they produce in your life, and above all, in God Himself (Romans 8:22–23; 5:2, 3, 11).

You Have Supernatural Help!

Another help in our worship (perhaps the major one) is the Holy Spirit, that wonderful Gift sent by our risen Lord to indwell us and empower us. The Lord has not set before us the ideal of a life filled with praise and then left us alone to achieve it. How could we, on our own, reach such a high goal—with the downward pull of our old fleshly patterns of living; with the pain of our trials, large or small; with our tendency to depend on ourselves and get distracted from the Lord and do our own thing? But we have the Holy Spirit! Just think of what this means!

He is within you as a fountain of water, springing up to fill you with fresh life—life that is eternal, life that is full. Through Him, time after time, you can know the refreshment that comes from the presence of the Lord. Through the Spirit you can understand the Scriptures and experience the marvelous things God has freely given you in Christ. Through Him you are linked in vital oneness with the Father and the Son and have all you need for life and godliness. You have all you need to inspire praise: comfort, encouragement, inexpressible joy, overflowing hope, strength in your innermost being, and power to love and serve.

You also have power to praise and give thanks: "Ever be filled with the Spirit...continue giving thanks for everything" (Ephesians 5:18, 20, Williams). You don't have to beg the Holy Spirit to fill you; He is eager to do so. You don't have to earn His fullness, proving you are worthy of it. You have only to let the Spirit fill you...to consent to live under His gracious influence and control. He then performs His amazing ministries in you. Among them: He inspires, reminds, and enables you to worship and praise and give thanks.

Praise Needs Cultivating

If God invites us to praise Him, if praise so enriches our experience of Him, and if we have the Holy Spirit indwelling us, why do we so easily neglect it? Why aren't we at all times attracted to praise as bees are to pollen?

I have worshiped the Lord for many years; I know how delightful praise is and how much it stimulates my faith. So why do I ever get so busy, even in my quiet time, that I bypass the delightful opportunity to extol and adore my wonderful Lord? Why do I, time and again, get so busy and absorbed with the pressures of daily life that I forget all about praise? And why do I at times feel reluctant to praise in the midst of everyday trials: when I hear news that makes me anxious about someone I love or when I face a major disappointment or when I'm angry or under a lot of pressure?

Could it be that one of Satan's major strategies is to divert us from praise? After all, he knows that God delights in our praise, and that doesn't exactly make him happy. He also detests the rich benefits praise brings to us and others. Or is it simply that our flesh prevails over our spirits, dampening our desire to glorify God? Might it be some of both?

Whatever the reason, we need to pray about a lifestyle of praise, as Horatio Bonar did a century ago:

Fill Thou my life, O Lord my God,
In every part with praise,
That my whole being may proclaim
Thy being and Thy ways.
Not for the lip of praise alone,
Nor e'en the praising heart
I ask, but for a life made up
Of praise in every part.

Or as the songwriter Robert Robinson prayed:

Come, Thou Fount of ev'ry blessing,
Tune my heart to sing Thy grace;
Streams of mercy, never ceasing,
Call for songs of loudest praise.

In spite of all that God has provided, including the Holy Spirit's presence and power, we don't automatically praise and give thanks. Nor will you find praise all of a sudden springing up in full bloom as soon as you start praying about it. Praise flourishes as you weed and water and fertilize your spiritual garden in which it grows. It becomes more constant as you nurture your soul on God's Word and walk in His ways, depending upon the Holy Spirit. It gets richer and more spontaneous as you grow in your knowledge of how worthy the Lord is to receive honor and glory and praise.

But even then praise does not *automatically* flow from your life day after day, hour after hour. You must choose to cultivate the habit of praise, taking steps that will enrich your praise life.

As you use the daily praises in this book, you'll find that praising God is an exciting adventure that yields rich dividends. The praise readings will help you make sense out of the hard realities of life. And—best of all—they'll deepen your experience of how vastly wonderful God is…how loving…how able to satisfy your heart and meet your deepest needs.

How to Use the Praise Pages

*Y*ou'll find each day of praise to be a rich way both to start your morning time with the Lord and to end your day, as you review each reading before bedtime. Underline the phrases that most touch your heart. Also put a mark by the things you need to accept with thanksgiving though you do not feel like it. Ask the Lord to do a special work in your heart in these areas.

Your response to some of the topics of praise may be, "How can I thank the Lord for that?" If these are your feelings, don't decide: *I guess these praise pages aren't for me.* Instead, pray about your response. If it's simply a matter of applying differently what you've learned from the Scriptures, feel free to express your praise in other words. But if you find an emotional block in your heart, seek to open yourself to the Lord on the issue that troubles you. In case He is putting His finger on something important, come back to that day of praise often, asking Him to do a new work within you.

I've personalized a great many of the passages that are quoted or referred to in the daily readings to help you use them in praise more easily. After each paragraph is a brief list of the scriptures quoted or referred to in that paragraph. You can become enriched and refreshed by looking up these scriptures in your Bible and meditating on them either before or after your time of praise.

In a notebook or journal, you may want to write out the passages that mean the most to you, along with any other special verses or thoughts that bless you.

Most Scripture references are taken from the New American Standard Bible, although many other versions and paraphrases are quoted as well, as indicated in the Scripture lists. (See the copyright page for the complete list of versions and their abbreviations.)

In your notebook or journal you may also want to record personal items about your life situation—things that will make your praise and thanksgiving broader, more meaningful to you—both enjoyable things and those issues you find difficult or painful. They will remind you to let God into your inner experience in new ways month after month.

Use the praise pages in an unhurried way, pausing now and then to let your heart quietly appreciate, adore, or stand in awe of your wonderful Lord. Take time to delight in who God is and bask in the sunshine of His presence.

You may also enjoy using these days of praise with a family member or friend, or for small-group study and discussion. The lists of Bible verses will be helpful for small-group study and discussion as you look up and reflect on these passages together.

Don't wait until after you've enjoyed all the praise pages to read the final section in this book, "Encouragement for a Lifetime of Praise." In this section you'll learn more about the rich and exciting ways your adventure in praise will reward you—a powerful enticement to continue praising month after month. You'll also find answers to some of your questions. And you'll gain insights that will add to your delight in many of the things you'll be praising the Lord for as you go through the days of praise.

Also, you may want to return often to the first daily reading, "Offering Myself: Your Most Basic Act of Worship." Use this one to renew your commitment to our wonderful Lord.

My longing is that the Lord will use this treasury of praise to help you especially in three ways: to experience God more fully in the varied needs and situations of your life, to be an increasing joy to Him, and to bring glory to His name in new ways.

Daily Praises — Part One

Cultivating a Life of Praise

Offering Myself

Your Most Basic Act of Worship

*L*ord, I'm Yours. Whatever the cost may be, may Your will be done in my life. I realize I'm not here on earth to do my own thing or to seek my own fulfillment or my own glory. I'm not here to indulge my desires, to increase my possessions, to impress people, to be popular, to prove I'm somebody important, or to promote myself. I'm not here even to be relevant or successful by human standards. I'm here to please You.

I offer myself to You, for You are worthy. All that I am or hope to be, I owe to You. I'm Yours by creation, and every day I receive from You life and breath and all things. And I'm Yours because You bought me, and the price You paid was the precious blood of Christ. You alone, the Triune God, are worthy to be my Lord and Master. I yield to You, my gracious and glorious heavenly Father; to the Lord Jesus who loved me and gave Himself for me; to the Holy Spirit and His gracious influence and empowering.

All that I am and all that I have I give to You.

I give You any rebellion in me, which resists doing Your will. I give You my pride and self-dependence, which tell me I can do Your will in my own power if I try hard enough. I give You my fears, which tell me I'll never be able to do Your will in some areas of life. I consent to let You energize me...to create within me, moment by moment, both the desire and the power to do Your will.

I give You my body and each of its members…my entire inner being: my mind, my emotional life, my will…my loved ones…my marriage or my hopes for marriage…my abilities and gifts…my strengths and weaknesses…my health…my status (high or low)…my possessions…my past, my present, and my future…when and how I'll go home to be with You.

I'm here to love You, to obey You, to glorify You. O my Beloved, may I be a joy to You!

All You Are

*M*y heart rejoices in You, Lord, for You are my strong shelter in times of trouble and danger and stress, my hiding place to whom I may *continually* resort…my Father who lovingly provides for me…my Shepherd who guides and protects me…my Champion who upholds my cause as His child and defends my highest interests…my Bridegroom who delights in me…my God who is mighty to save, who rests in His love for me and rejoices over me with singing, with shouts of joy. You are my inheritance, my share in life, the One who satisfies my longing soul and fills my hungry soul with goodness.

Psalms 71:3; 91:1-2; 27:5; Matthew 6:25-26; Psalm 23:1-3; Isaiah 19:20; 62:5b;
Zephaniah 3:17-18; Psalms 16:5-6; 107:9

I praise You for Your love and Your wisdom. You are too wise to ever make a mistake, too loving to ever do anything unkind. You act on my behalf, accomplishing what concerns me and fulfilling Your purpose for me as I call on You. Thank You that You love me deeply and tenderly. You are compassionate and gracious, full of lovingkindness, ready to forgive, patiently considerate, and generous beyond imagining. You desire my love and rejoice to do good things for me. You delight to give me the desires of my heart as I delight myself in You. How precious is Your love to me, O God! I sing for joy as I take refuge in the shadow of Your wings!

Psalms 57:2; 138:8; 103:8; 86:5; Matthew 22:37; Jeremiah 32:41; Psalms 37:4; 63:7; 36:7

Your Son

*T*hank You, Father, that You so loved the world that You gave Your one and only Son, our Lord Jesus Christ…that when the time had fully come, He wrapped Himself in human form, being born as a helpless baby in a poor family. Thank You that He walked here on earth, radiating the brightness of Your glory and flawlessly expressing Your nature…and so, through Him, people saw You in action, involved with them, available to meet their needs. Thank You that He focused Your almighty power into the lives of common people with deep needs, just like me…that He preached the gospel to the poor, proclaimed freedom to prisoners of sin and recovery of sight to the blind, and set free the oppressed victims of sin and Satan—the downtrodden, the lost, the hurting, the broken. Thank You for the way He rebuked the arrogant and looked with favor on the humble-minded, opening wide the door of His kingdom to those who were destitute and helpless in spirit. I delight in Your tender mercies, O my God, by which the Sunrise from on high has come to us!

John 3:16; Galatians 4:4; Hebrews 1:3; Luke 4:18-19; Matthew 5:3; Luke 1:78

Thank You that through the Gospels I can watch this beloved One walk among ordinary people. I can hear the gracious words that came from His lips. I can see His compassion and tenderness toward needy people, His anger at hypocrisy, His faithfulness, His intense love for His followers.

Luke 4:22; Matthew 9:36; 15:32; 23:37; 23:13-33; John 13:1

Fairest Lord Jesus! You alone are my heart's desire...my chief delight... my soul's glory, joy, and crown. Every advantage life can offer is like rubbish, compared with the overwhelming gain of knowing You. You are worthy, Lord—worthy to be thanked and praised and worshiped and adored.

Psalm 45:2; Song of Solomon 5:16; Philippians 3:8 Phillips

Christ's Life on Earth

I praise You that the Lord Jesus lived His life sinlessly, in total accord with reality, with no falseness, no self-deception, no dark secrets, nothing to regret, nothing to be ashamed of…that He proclaimed the truth, the one utterly reliable foundation for our thinking and living. Thank You that He delighted to do Your will…that He withdrew for time alone in Your presence…that He was attentive to Your voice and sensitive to Your working…that He lived in complete dependence on You so that You in Him spoke those gracious and life-giving words and performed those mighty works.

Hebrews 4:15; Matthew 7:24-28; Psalm 40:8; Mark 1:35;

Luke 5:16; Isaiah 50:4; John 5:19; 6:57; 14:10

Thank You that He demonstrated how I am to live and serve, completely depending on Him as my indwelling Lord, focusing on His life as He walked on earth, and beholding His glory, "the glory of the One and Only" who came from You, full of grace and truth. What a delight to know that as I focus on Him, You transform me into His image by Your Spirit within me. You work in me that which is pleasing in Your eyes. You strengthen my heart in every good work and every good word so that more and more I honor Christ by the way I live.

John 15:5; 1:14 NIV; 2 Corinthians 3:18; Hebrews 13:21;

2 Thessalonians 2:17; Philippians 1:20 Phillips

My Savior

I love You, Father, because You first loved me and sent Your Son to atone for my sins. And I stand amazed that Jesus, who by nature had always been God, did not cling to His rights as Your equal...that He laid aside all His privileges to be born as a human being...that He totally humbled Himself, submitting to the death of a common criminal, enduring infinite humiliation and pain...that on the cross You laid on Him the compressed weight of all my sin and guilt and shame, all my griefs and sorrows, and He became sin for me, dying the death I deserved.

1 John 4:10; Philippians 2:6-9; Isaiah 53:3-12; 2 Corinthians 5:21

And how much I praise You that it was impossible for death to hold Him in its power...that You raised Him from the dead to be my Savior, to make me righteous in Your sight...that You highly exalted Him, giving Him a position infinitely superior to any conceivable command, authority, power, or control, both natural and supernatural. Thank You that He is the Great High Priest...that He is able to save me completely, for He lives forever and prays for me and for all of us who have come to You through Him. I glorify You, my Father, with gratefulness and joy.

Acts 2:24; Romans 4:24 NIV; Ephesians 1:20-22 Phillips; Hebrews 8:1; 7:25

And I bow at the feet of Him who was dead and is now alive forever and ever. I exalt Him, I yield myself to Him, for He is worthy of the total response of my entire being: "Worthy is the Lamb that was slain to receive power and riches and wisdom and might and honor and glory and blessing."

Revelation 1:18; 5:12

Your Majesty
and Sovereignty

I magnify You, O Lord, I exalt Your name, for You are great and highly to be praised. I praise You for the glorious splendor of Your majesty and the power of Your awe-inspiring acts. Your power is unlimited...absolute...beyond imagining. You are able to do immeasurably more than we can ask or dream of. "There is nothing too hard for You." Who is like You, "majestic in holiness, awesome in praises, working wonders"?

Psalm 145:3-6; Ephesians 3:20; Jeremiah 32:17 NKJV; Exodus 15:11

O Lord Most High, You rule over the heavens and the earth, for You made all things by Your great power, and You keep them existing and working by Your mighty Word. You are exalted high above every star and galaxy in the entire cosmos...yet You are also "the God of all mankind," the great, personally present, personally involved God who loves, rescues, and takes care of all who trust You. You exercise Your gracious authority over all nations—and over each individual in all the world. There is none like You, the true God, the living God, the everlasting King.

Hebrews 1:3; Jeremiah 32:27 NIV; 10:6-7

I praise You for Your sovereignty over the broad events of my life and over the details. With You, nothing is accidental, nothing is incidental, and no experience is wasted. You hold in Your own power my breath of life and all my destiny. And every trial that You allow to happen is a platform on which You reveal Yourself, showing Your love and power, both to me and to others looking on. Thank You that I can move into the future nondefensively, with hands outstretched to whatever lies ahead, for You hold the future and You will always be with me, even to my old age…and through all eternity.

Daniel 5:23d; Hebrews 13:5; Isaiah 46:4

Christ's Return

I magnify You, my God, for Your absolute purity, holiness, and justice, as the Judge to whom all people must give account. I praise You that Your fairness is intertwined with everything You do...that when the time is ripe, You will end all sin and injustice, all corruption, all immorality...that You will right all wrongs and reward all loving service and suffering for Your sake.

Psalm 99:3,9; Daniel 4:37; Romans 14:12; Deuteronomy 32:4;
Isaiah 2:10-12; Romans 12:19; Hebrews 6:10

Thank You that Your Son will return from heaven with a shout of triumph, that the dead in Christ will be raised imperishable...and in a flash, in the twinkling of an eye, we shall all be utterly changed. We shall see the radiance of His face and the glorious majesty of His power. It will be a breathtaking wonder and splendor unimaginable to all who believe! Thank You that "whatever we may have to go through now is less than nothing compared with the magnificent future" You have planned for us.

I Thessalonians 4:16; I Corinthians 15:51-52; 2 Thessalonians 1:6-10 Phillips; Romans 8:18 Phillips

What a joy it is to know that the government will be on Christ's shoulders and that there will be no end to the increase of His government and peace...that His kingdom will be established with justice and righteousness from then on and forevermore. Your kingdom is an everlasting kingdom…a kingdom that cannot be shaken. You will never be voted out; no coup will ever dethrone You. For all eternity You are the King of kings and Lord of lords. To You "be the glory and the dominion forever and ever. Amen"!

Isaiah 9:6-7; Daniel 4:34; Hebrews 12:28; 1 Timothy 6:15; Revelation 19:6; 1:6

Your Word

I glorify You for the Bible—that wonderful, written revelation of You and Your plan. As snow and rain fall from the skies to meet our needs, so You have condensed Your thoughts—which are vastly higher than all human thoughts—into written form. I'm so grateful that You cared enough to communicate with us in this clear, unchanging, always-accessible way so that Your thoughts are now available at all times to refresh and nourish and teach me…and that You are still a communicating God, speaking these words to me as I am attentive to You, as I read and meditate with a listening heart. What a privilege it is to store Your Word in my heart, where You can use it at any moment to bless me and guide me…to keep me from sinning against You…and to be a storehouse of inspired words that the Spirit can bring to my mind to help others.

Isaiah 55:8-11; Psalm 119:11

Thank You that in Your Word I can see Your face and hear Your voice. I can discover Your will and Your patterns for living and serving. I can develop deeper faith and confidence. Thank You that the Holy Spirit inspired Your Word and uses it to enlighten and guide me and to change me more and more into Your image, from one degree of glory to another.

2 Peter 1:20-21; 2 Timothy 3:16-17

How I'm Created

I give thanks to You, O Lord, and I stand in awe of You, for I am wonderfully made. Marvelous are Your works! Thank You that You uniquely designed and created me with the same care and precision You used in creating the universe...that You formed me in love exactly to Your specifications...that You embroidered me with great skill in my mother's womb. I kneel before You, my Maker.

Psalms 139:13-16; 95:6

I'm grateful that my looks, my abilities, and my personality are like a special picture frame in which You can portray Your grace and beauty, Your love, Your strength, Your faithfulness, to the praise of Your glory. I rejoice that You have gifted me for the special purposes You have in mind for my life. I thank You for Your loving wisdom in allowing the things that have influenced me throughout my life—the things that have prepared my heart to respond to You and live for Your glory. I might not have turned to You if things had been different!

Ephesians 1:6,12; Romans 12:3-6; Psalm 119:67,71

It's wonderful to know that You are not the least bit dissatisfied with my inborn talents, intelligence, aptitudes, appearance, and personality, for Your hands have made and fashioned me. I am one of Your original masterpieces!

Psalm 119:73

My Gifts

I worship before You, dear Lord, as the all-wise Creator, the One who made heaven and earth and all that is in them and saw that it was very good. I praise You for the honor of being made in Your image, personally formed by You for Your glory, and gifted spiritually just as it has pleased You. Thank You for each strength and ability and desirable trait You have given me. Surely You have been good to me, O Lord!

Genesis 1:31,27; Isaiah 43:7; Psalm 8:3-6

Thank You that I can enjoy my strengths and gifts without pride or false modesty as I give You the credit for them, praising You rather than congratulating myself. What do I have that I did not receive from You?... All that I am and all that I have comes from You; it is all sustained by You...and I want it all to glorify You! Not to me, O Lord, not to me, but to Your name be the glory.

Romans 12:3-6; John 3:27; 1 Corinthians 4:7; 1 Peter 4:10; Romans 11:36; Psalm 115:1 NIV

I specifically thank You for:

My Weaknesses

I choose to thank You for my weaknesses, my infirmities, my in-adequacies (physical, mental, emotional, relational)…for the ways I fall short of what people view as ideal…for my feelings of help-lessness and inferiority and even my pain and distresses. What a comfort it is to know that You understand the feeling of my weaknesses!…and that in Your infinite wisdom You have allowed these in my life so that they may contribute to Your high purposes for me.

Hebrews 4:15; Romans 8:28-29

Thank You that many a time my weaknesses cut through my pride and help me walk humbly with You…and then, as You've promised, You give me more grace—You help and bless and strengthen me. Thank You for all the ways I'm inadequate, for they prod me to trust in You and not in myself…and I'm grateful that my adequacy comes from You, the all-sufficient God who is enough!

James 4:6; Psalm 40:17; 2 Corinthians 12:7-10; 3:5

Thank You that I can trust You to remove or change any of my weaknesses and handicaps and shortcomings the moment they are no longer needed for Your glory, and for my good, and for the good of other people…and that in the meantime, Your grace is sufficient for me, for Your strength is made perfect in my weakness.

2 Corinthians 12:7-10

Your Plan for Me

*T*hank You, my gracious and sovereign God, that You have been with me and carried me from the day of my birth until today…that You have known my whole life, from beginning to end, since before I was born…and that You wrote in Your book all the days that You ordained for me before one of them came to be.

Isaiah 46:3,9-10; Psalm 139:16

Thank You that in Your gracious plan to bless and use me, You've allowed me to go through hard times, through trials that many people go through in this fallen world. How glad I am that You're so good at reaching down and making something beautiful out of even the worst situations! How encouraged I am when I think how You did this for Joseph…how his brothers hated and abused and betrayed him, and how You worked these things out for blessing, both for Joseph and his family and for countless other people.

Hebrews 10:34; 1 Peter 5:9; Genesis 37; 50:17-20

I praise You that the things that happened in my past, both enjoyable and painful, are raw materials for blessings, both in my life and in the lives of others. So I thank You for the specific family (or lack of family) into which I was born and the opportunities You did or did not provide. And thank You for the things in my past that appear to be limitations, hindrances, bad breaks…the wounds of old hurts, the unmet emotional needs, the mistakes or neglect of other people—even their cruelty to me, their abuse.

I Thessalonians 5:18

How comforting to know that in all my distresses You were distressed. And how I thank You, Lord Jesus, that on the cross You bore my griefs and carried my sorrows as well as my sins...that I can kneel at the cross and worship You as the One who took on Yourself all my pain and experienced it to the full. And how comforting to know that in the present, day by day, You feel with me any pain, confusion, inner bondage, or struggles that stem from my past. Thank You that all these seeming disadvantages are a backdrop for the special, unfolding plan You have in mind for me...and that if my past still handicaps me, You are able to lead me to the kind of help I need.

Isaiah 63:9; 53:4

I'm so grateful that all my past circumstances were permitted by You to make me see my need of You and prepare my heart for Your Word...to draw me to Yourself and to work out Your good purposes for my life. I rejoice that You are the Blessed Controller of all things—You are now, You will be throughout the future, and You always were. All my days had Your touch of love and wisdom whether or not I can as yet fully see it.

Deuteronomy 8:3; Psalm 66:6-12; I Timothy 6:15 Phillips

And Lord, I choose to look beyond my past and present troubles in this life—this temporary life—and fix my eyes on the unseen things that will last forever. I praise You for the eternal glory these things are piling up for me as I choose to trust You.

2 Corinthians 4:17-18

Righteousness

I glory in Your holy name, dear Lord, for in Christ I am righteous
with His righteousness. I am justified—just as if I'd never
sinned! I'm totally right with You!… Thank You that on the cross Jesus
bore all the guilt of all my sins, including past and present and future
ones. How grateful I am that, because of what Jesus did, "You crossed out
the whole debt against me in Your account books. You nailed the account
book to the cross, and closed the account."

1 Corinthians 1:30; 2 Corinthians 5:21; Romans 5:1; Isaiah 53:6; Colossians 2:14 Laubach

Now, Father, I bow before You as the Judge to whom I am accountable as the final Authority, the Chief Justice of the Supreme Court
of all the earth…and I thank You, I praise You that You have said—and
Your Word cannot be broken—"No condemnation now hangs over the
head of those who are 'in' Christ Jesus.… God himself has declared us
free from sin."

Romans 14:12; Psalms 50:6; 96:13; Romans 8:1,33 Phillips

How I rejoice that through Christ I am all right as a person, now and
forever: totally clean, every stain removed…totally forgiven, no matter
how great or recent a failure I've had to confess or how often I have failed.

Hebrews 10:14; Titus 3:4-5; John 13:10; Psalm 130:3-4; Romans 7:18-20,25

What amazing grace! What undeserved acceptance and favor! How wonderful that You ask me to do absolutely nothing to earn Your forgiveness—no striving to measure up, no self-punishment, no prolonged remorse, no self-blame, no deeds of penance...that I don't have to sink down into regrets, or into shame, or into denial, or into excuses for things I do wrong. I'm so thankful that You don't hold a pair of scales and ask me to pile up enough good works to outweigh my sins, my failures, my unworthiness...that it's all by grace through faith. What an incentive to live a life that pleases You, that brings You joy and not grief!

Ephesians 2:8-9; Psalm 103:10-14; Romans 4:7-8; 11:6; 6:1-2; Ephesians 2:10

I greatly rejoice in You, Lord; my soul exults in You; for You have clothed me with the garments of salvation, You have wrapped me with a robe of righteousness and beauty, as a bridegroom dressed for his wedding, as a bride adorned with her jewels.

Isaiah 61:10

Belonging

I magnify You with thanksgiving, my Father, for I belong to You forever. You chose me in Christ before the creation of the world. You drew me to Yourself. You accepted me in Your beloved Son, welcoming me into the everlasting love You have for Him...and now You take me, as Your child, in Your arms and tell me that You love me.

Ephesians 1:4; John 6:44; Ephesians 1:6 KJV; John 17:23; Hosea 11:3; Isaiah 43:4

Thank You that I have a place in You and Your kingdom that is eternal...that nothing can separate me from Your limitless, intensely personal love—the one love that is not the least bit based on how much I deserve it, the one love that can never lessen or fail. Thank You that You will never be disillusioned with me, for You already know all about me: past, present, and future.

Colossians 1:12; Jeremiah 31:3; Romans 8:38-39; Psalm 139:1-6

How great is Your love toward me, Father, that I should be called Your child, and such I am. How amazing that I am precious in Your eyes and that You love me!

1 John 3:1; Isaiah 43:4

The Holy Spirit

*F*ather, I'm so glad that the Holy Spirit is within me, to strengthen me with power in my inner person...to make Christ real within me and flood my heart with His limitless love...to fill me with Your fullness...to enable me to know in personal experience the things You have so freely bestowed on me in Christ—my new identity, my incredible spiritual blessings.

Romans 8:9-10; Ephesians 3:16-19

I celebrate the fact that I have been crucified with Christ and that now I am alive with His life...that through my new birth I died out of my old life and that You resurrected me to a living relationship with You...and so I am dead to sin and alive to You! Thank You that these facts are true, whether or not they seem logical, whether or not I feel they're true...and that as I praise You for them, Your Spirit enables me more and more to live in the light of my new identity in You. Thank You that He is using Your Word to deliver me from the viewpoints and values of the world, the flesh, and the devil...and He is renewing my mind to see things from Your point of view so I can walk in newness of life.

Galatians 2:20; 6:14; Romans 6:1-11

I praise You that Christ is not a weak person outside me but a tremendous power inside me...that through Him I am competent to cope with life, to do Your will, to love with Your love, to be more than a conqueror.

How I rejoice that I can grow, develop my gifts, enlarge my capacities...that I need not be forever shackled by my past but that with confidence and joy I can look forward to actually becoming all You have in mind for me to be.

2 Corinthians 13:3 Phillips; Philippians 4:13; Romans 8:37

Christt at Work Within Me

I'm so grateful, Lord, that the Christian life is not a rigorous self-improvement course or a do-it-yourself kit...that it is not a call to prove myself or improve myself by overcoming my own shortcomings and failures, in my own way, by my own resources. Thank You that, instead, You are at work in me and in my situation to break old patterns of thought and action, to create within me both the desire and the power to do Your gracious will...and to make me a joy to You in new ways.

John 15:5; Philippians 2:13

I praise You that "Jesus Christ is able to untangle all the snarls in my soul, to banish all my complexes, and to transform even my fixed habit patterns, no matter how deeply they are etched in my subconscious" (Corrie ten Boom). Thank You for the many ways You use other people to counsel me and help me grow...and yet that Christ Himself is the Answer to my hang-ups, the one Source who can meet my deepest needs. How I rejoice that He is wonderful in counsel and mighty in power and that He heals from the inside out.

Hebrews 10:24-25; Ephesians 4:16 TLB; John 6:35; 7:37-38; 8:12; Isaiah 9:6; 28:29

Thank You, too, for the Holy Spirit—the Spirit of wisdom and understanding, the Spirit of counsel and strength. I praise You that He is in me to enlighten me through Your Word, to flush away my anxieties and fears, my resentments and hostilities, my guilt and regrets, as water flushes away dirt and trash…to keep me filled with Himself and to flood my heart with Your love…to produce through me the fruit of love, joy, peace, patience, kindness, goodness, faithfulness, gentleness, and self-control…and to enable me to give thanks for all things as the hours and days and weeks pass. I rejoice that You are able to do far more than all I ask or think, according to Your power that is at work within me—the same power that raised Jesus from the dead!

Isaiah 11:2; John 16:13; Ephesians 5:18-20; Romans 5:5 Phillips;

Galatians 5:22-23; Ephesians 3:20; 1:19-21

Honor, Favor, Significance

hank You, dear Lord, that I am honored in Your eyes…that even the person who is least in Your kingdom is greater in Your sight than the most prominent and successful person ever born. How wonderful that You, the high King of heaven, enthroned far above all other powers in heaven and earth, have bestowed on me the royal dignity of being Your child and heir!

Isaiah 43:4; Matthew 11:11; Romans 8:16-17

I exult in Your marvelous grace—in Your favor and blessings, which I do not deserve—for You have raised me up with Christ and seated me with Him in the heavenly realm, far above any conceivable command, authority, power, or control. You have given me an exalted status in Your kingdom—in the one realm where being included and honored has any real significance, any lasting value.

Ephesians 2:6; 1:20-21

How grateful I am that You have linked me to the greatest possible purposes, the highest of all reasons for living: to know and love You…to show Your love to other people…to glorify You…and to enjoy You now and forever. What an honor!

John 17:3; Matthew 22:37-38; 1 Peter 4:8-11; Isaiah 43:7; John 17:24

Thank You that, in my deepest and truest identity, I am a new person in union with Christ...that I am one of Your spiritual masterpieces, created clean and clear as a flawless jewel...and that You are cutting and polishing me to receive and display more fully the beauty of Your glorious attributes!

2 Corinthians 5:17; Ephesians 2:10; I Peter 2:9

Where I Am

hank You that You have me in the place You want me just now…that even if I got here through wrong choices or in-difference or even rebellion, You knew my mistakes and sins before I ever existed, and You worked them into Your plan to draw me to Your-self, to mold and bless me and to bless others through me. Thank You that, even if I'm here through the ill will or poor judgment of other peo-ple, all is well; for in Your sovereign wisdom You are at work to bring about good results from all those past decisions, those past events beyond my control—good results both for me and for others. Thank You again that You meant for good the terrible things that happened to Joseph, who was sold into slavery, exiled to a distant country, and later sent to prison on false accusations…and that through all this You had him in the right place at the right time for highly important reasons. I'm glad, Lord, that You are the same today—well able to work things out for us, to turn evil into good. I stand amazed at the complexity and mystery of Your wisdom. How safe it is for me to trust Your reasons for acting (or not acting) and Your methods of working!

Isaiah 46:9; Genesis 37; 39; Psalm 105:16-20; Genesis 50:20; Romans 11:33 Phillips

Thank You that I can safely commit my location and situation to You. I can "be willing for You to shift me anywhere on life's checkerboard, or bury me anywhere in life's garden, gladly yielding myself for You to please

Yourself with, anywhere and any way You choose" (source unknown). Thank You that I can trust You with my future places—ready to go, ready to stay.

Psalms 37:5; 73:24; Revelation 3:7-8

So I rest in the fact that You have me in this place for this day, and I praise You that You will faithfully guide me throughout life to just where You want me to be, as I seek to do Your will.

Deuteronomy 1:33

And most important of all is my place in You. How delighted I am to have You as my dwelling place where I can settle down, feel secure, and be content anywhere on earth. You are my blessed home, "where I can enter and be at rest even when all around and above is a sea of trouble" (Andrew Murray). How my soul delights to hide in the secret of Your presence…to take refuge in the shadow of Your wings, to eat at Your table, to drink my fill of the river of Your delights. How blessed I am, my King and my God, for You have chosen me and brought me near, to live in Your presence, to behold Your delightfulness, to seek Your counsel… And to think that I will dwell in Your house forever!

Psalms 90:1; 91:1; 31:20; 36:7-8; 65:4; 27:4-5; 23:6

Disappointments and Struggles

*F*ather, I'm so delighted that You are both loving and sovereign and that You cause all things to work together for good to those who love You, to those who are called according to Your purpose. So I thank You for each disturbing or humbling situation in my life, for each breaking or cleansing process You are allowing, for each problem or hindrance, for each thing that triggers in me anxiety or anger or pain. And I thank You in advance for each disappointment, each demanding duty, each pressure, each interruption that may arise in the coming hours and days.

Romans 8:28-29; 1 Peter 1:6-7

In spite of what I think or feel when I get my eyes off You, I choose not to resist my trials as intruders but to welcome them as friends.

James 1:2-4 Phillips

Thank You that each difficulty is an opportunity to see You work…that in Your time You will bring me out to a place of abundance. I rejoice that You plan to enrich and beautify me through each problem, each conflict, each struggle…that through them You expose my weaknesses and needs, my hidden sins, my self-centeredness (and especially my self-reliance and pride). Thank You that You use trials to humble me and perfect my faith and produce in me the quality of endurance...that they prepare the soil of my heart for the fresh new growth in godliness that You and I both long to see in me...and that my momentary troubles are producing for me an eternal glory that far outweighs them all, as I keep my eyes focused on You. I'm grateful that You look beyond my superficial desire for a trouble-free life; instead, You fulfill my deep-down desire to glorify You, enjoy Your warm fellowship, and become more like Your Son.

Psalms 68:8-12; 138:7-8; Job 23:10; Deuteronomy 8:2-3,16-17;

2 Corinthians 4:17-18; John 12:27-28

People Who Bless Me

hank You, Lord, for the people who are a blessing to me…for family and friends and neighbors, for little children, for brothers and sisters in Christ, for colleagues and leaders, for pastors and teachers…and for others: our doctor, the postman, the plumber. Thank You for the many ways You use these people to meet my needs, brighten my path, and lighten my load…to enrich my knowledge of You and to counsel or correct or nourish me, building me up in the faith. How good and how pleasant it is to enjoy rich fellowship with those who love You. Thank You for bringing people into my life!

Philippians 1:3; 1 Thessalonians 2:19-20; Psalm 68:6a; Ephesians 4:11-16;

Galatians 6:10; Matthew 22:39; 1 John 4:11-12; Psalm 133:1

I thank You *specifically* for:

Yet, Lord, I also thank You that even the people I most admire have flaws—that only You are wonderful through and through, with no ugly edges, and that people, even at their best, cannot meet my deepest needs…that at times they misunderstand, they disappoint, they expect too much, or they can't be available when I need them. This makes me even more glad to have You as my best Friend, my wonderful Counselor, my ever-present help in trouble, immediately available around the clock, seven days a week. How wonderful that I belong to You, the pure, unpolluted Source from which all downstream loves flow. So I delight in people here on earth, but first and last, I come to You, the only perfect Person, the only ideal Person, the only One whose love is flawless...the only One who is worthy of my highest praise. O God, who is like You? There is none to compare with You!

Isaiah 9:6; Psalm 46:1; 1 John 4:10,18-19; Psalm 45:2; Hebrews 7:26; Psalm 40:5b

People Who Bring Pain

*F*ather, I thank You for the people in my life who seem to bring more pain than joy, for I believe You have let our paths cross for important reasons. Thank You for the good things You want to do in my life through the things that bother me (their irritating habits? their moodiness? their unloving ways? their demands? their insensitivity? their unrealistic expectations?). I'm grateful that You are with me to meet my needs when others—even those close to me—fail to do so. I'm so glad that You are also within me, working to make me more like Jesus—more patient, more gentle, more loving—through the very things I dislike.

Romans 8:28-29; 1 Peter 1:6-7; James 1:2-4 Phillips; Psalm 27:10; Isaiah 49:14-16;
Psalm 142:3-5; 1 Thessalonians 3:12; Philippians 1:9-11

Thank You, too, that You love these people and that Your love is adequate to meet their deep needs and to transform their lives, however willful or unwise they may sometimes be. Thank You that You care for them deeply and that each of them has the potential of being a vast reservoir from which You could receive eternal pleasure. And so, though I may not feel grateful, I give thanks for them by faith, trusting Your goodness, Your wisdom, Your power, and Your love for them as well as for me.

Matthew 5:43-45; Hosea 3:1

And I praise You that I need not fret about these people, or be envious, or mull over angry thoughts to prove I'm right. Thank You that by

Your power I can receive them as You receive me—just as I am, warts and wrinkles and hang-ups and all—that I can choose not to judge them but to forgive them…to cancel any debts I feel they owe me—any apologies, any obligations—that through Your grace I can choose to wipe clean any slate of grievances I have within me and view these people with a heart that says, "You no longer owe me a thing." Thank You for Your Spirit who empowers me so I can do them good, delight in You, and commit my way to You, resting in You as You unfold Your good purposes in these relationships—in Your time.

1 Peter 2:1; Romans 15:7; Ephesians 4:31-32; Matthew 7:1-3; 6:14-15; 18:21-22; Psalm 37:1-7

My Life Partner

*T*hank You, Lord, for each specific strong point and admirable quality in my life partner.* Thank You for bringing us together and for the way Your love sweetens our earthly love! I bless You, Lord, for the many benefits You have given me through this dear one.

Psalms 103:1-2; 128:1-4

Here are some special reasons I want to thank You for this relationship:

Yet, Lord, I praise You that You far surpass even the best person in my life. You are distinguished above all, "the most winsome of all beings" (Tozer). You are my share in life, my reward, my inheritance.

Psalms 73:25; 45:2; Song of Solomon 5:10; Psalm 16:5-6

Who can compare with You? You are my perfect Life Partner, my dearest, most delightful Loved One, my always-present Companion. You are the strength of my life and my portion forever. Only my relationship with You is sure to be lifelong and more, with never a good-bye!

Psalm 89:5-17; Jeremiah 10:6-7; 2 Corinthians 11:2; Isaiah 54:5; Psalm 73:25-26; Hosea 2:19-20

---

* If you are married, make your partner the topic of your praise. If you are not married, choose another person who is close to you: a family member, roommate, or friend. Give thanks for that person's good qualities—even if right now you find it difficult to focus on those good points.

Thank You that "You are so vastly wonderful, so utterly and completely delightful, that You can meet and overflow the deepest demands of my total nature, mysterious and deep as that nature is" (Tozer).

Psalms 107:8-9; 37:4; 84:11; Isaiah 55:1-2

Thank You for Your ultimate good purposes in allowing my life partner's weaknesses or failures (indifference? lack of understanding? harshness? explosiveness? undue need to control? excessive dependence? excessive independence? failure to lead, failure to follow, failure to love? lack of alertness and awareness? other lacks or failures or even grievous sins?).

1 Thessalonians 5:18

I especially want to thank You for what You plan to do through the things that disappoint me, upset me, make me anxious, or break my heart.

Hebrews 12:10-11

Thank You for Your ultimate good purposes in allowing these things. And thank You so much that these things do not make up the whole picture—that this loved one is also wonderfully made and has a bright side as well as a dull side. And I rejoice that You are loving and powerful, well able to change this person if and when and as You choose. Thank You that in the meantime You are working to change me through these imperfections that frustrate or grieve me…that my reactions to them throw light on ways I need to grow—to trust You more—and to meet my loved one's needs more fully as I let the Holy Spirit fill me with Your love and patience and peace.

Psalm 139:14; Jeremiah 32:17,27; Romans 4:17; Proverbs 3:5;

1 Peter 3:1-9; Philippians 1:9-10; Galatians 5:22-23

I rejoice that You are able to empower me in difficult times and to give me wisdom in my responses. You are all-sufficient, more than enough to meet even the deepest needs of my heart, whatever today or the future may bring.

James 1:5; Psalms 73:25-26; 90:14

Loved Ones in Their Trials

hank You that You plan to use for good the struggles my loved ones face—including their disappointing choices, their unwise or even harmful ways of thinking and living, and their sidetracks from going Your way (as I see it—and, Lord, I know I could be wrong!).

Romans 8:28-29

I praise You in advance for the part these difficult things are going to play in Your good plan for us—in eventual deliverance and growth and fruitfulness. I'm grateful that in all these things the battle is not mine but Yours...and that the final chapter has not yet been written. How good it is that I can call on You to give me wisdom to know what to say or not say, what to do or not do...and that You live in me so that I can love with Your love, even when it's hard. Thank You that these trials force me to trust You more!

James 1:2-4 Phillips; 2 Chronicles 20:15; James 1:5,19-20; 3:17-18; Ecclesiastes 3:7

I worship before You, my King and my God. I'm grateful that You command victories for Your people...and that "all things are thy servants." You're a God who acts on behalf of the one who puts his hope in You. Thank You that You are at work to answer my prayers in Your good way and time.

Psalms 44:4; 119:91 RSV; Isaiah 66:14

Thank You for past victories You have won in my loved ones' lives—for progress and growth and answered prayer—and for the victories we will yet see in the future, to the glory of Your Name. I praise You that, as time goes by, in new ways You will show us Your goodness in the land of the living.

Psalm 27:13

My Failures, Sins, Mistakes

*T*hank You, my loving and sovereign God, that my failures and mistakes are part of the "all things" You work together for good—as well as my tensions and stresses, my hostile and anxious feelings, my regrets, my trips into shame and self-blame, and the specific things that trigger them. I praise You that "all things," including these, can contribute to my spiritual growth and my experience of You. When my heart is overwhelmed, I'm more aware of my need to cry to You…to take refuge in You…to rely on You.

Romans 8:28-29; Psalm 61:2

I rejoice that these things keep reminding me to depend on You with all my heart…that they prompt me to trust in Your love, Your forgiveness, Your power, Your sufficiency, Your ability to overrule, and Your transforming presence within me. Thank You for the ways that my shortcomings and failures bring pressure on me to open myself to You more fully and the way they let You show me deep and hidden needs: griefs and hurts that I've never poured out before You, that I've never exposed to Your healing touch, and sins that I've never faced and acknowledged. How grateful I am for Your constant cleansing as I confess each sin You make me aware of and then turn back to You as my Lord. I praise You that I'm free from condemnation simply because Christ died for me and rose again…that it doesn't depend on how well I live.

Proverbs 3:5; Psalm 37:5; 2 Corinthians 3:18; 1 John 1:9

I praise You for how You use my sins and failures to humble me and for how this opens me to the inflow of Your grace—amazing grace that enables me to hold my head high, not in pride, but in humble gratitude for Your undeserved, unchanging love and total cleansing!

I Peter 5:5-6; Romans 5:5 TLB

Position and Performance

*D*ear Lord, how much I appreciate Your viewpoint regarding human status and abilities, failures and weaknesses. I'm so glad that You, the high and exalted One, are not impressed with the positions people hold...that You are not in the least partial or prejudiced...that You show no personal favoritism. Thank You that You have no regard for any external distinctions: for rich or poor, for famous or unknown, for high rank or low, for handsome or homely, for any race or culture above any other...but that You do have regard for all who are humble in heart. Thank You that You are not looking for ideal people with imposing lists of human qualifications but that You use people whom the world calls foolish and weak, poor and insignificant. Thank You that You oppose those who exalt themselves and that You exalt those who humble themselves, giving them Your grace.

Isaiah 57:15; Galatians 2:6; James 2:1,5; 1 Corinthians 1:26-29; James 4:6; Psalm 73:1-18

How glad I am that You don't expect perfect performance. "You are quick to mark every simple effort to please You, and just as quick to overlook imperfections when I meant to do Your will" (Tozer). You are full of mercy and compassion toward me. You know the way I'm put together; You know my limitations; You understand that I am dust. And I praise You that You are greater than any or all of my failures...that as my Potter, You are able to mold and remold me as I submit to Your wisdom and skill...that as the Master Artist, You are able to take the dark threads of my life—my wounds, my scars, my blotches, the messes I make, and even my sins—and blend them into a beautiful design to the praise of the glory of Your grace.

Psalm 103:13-14; Jeremiah 18:3-6

Thank You that I, a common earthenware jug, contain the priceless treasure of Your life and glory, so my every victory and accomplishment obviously comes from Your all-prevailing power and not from me.

2 Corinthians 4:7

Victory in Christ

*F*ather, I praise You that Jesus is Victor over Satan and all his evil powers—that He triumphed over them through the Cross and Resurrection, and that You have highly exalted Him. You have given Him a position infinitely superior to all other powers and authorities...a name that stands far above all other names that will ever be used, and— amazing grace—You have raised me up and enthroned me with Him in the heavenly realms.

Colossians 2:15; Ephesians 1:19-21; Philippians 2:9-10; Ephesians 2:6

How I praise You that I need not strive toward a possible victory but can live from a position of victory already won—that He who is in me (Father, Son, and Holy Spirit) is greater than he who is in the world...that although Satan is powerful, he cannot prevail against the blood of the Lamb and the Name of our Lord Jesus Christ. Thank You that Satan must retreat before that Name and before Your Word, the living and powerful sword of the Spirit, and that in the end he will be cast down into everlasting defeat and shame.

1 John 4:4; Revelation 12:11; Acts 16:18; Ephesians 6:17; Revelation 20:10

What a joy to know that You are the same today as You were centuries ago in Isaiah's day, when You promised to rescue Your people from a hopeless-looking situation, when the enemy seemed to have prevailed. How I love the words You spoke to them: "Those who hopefully wait for

Me will not be put to shame.... Even the captives of the mighty man will be taken away, and the prey of the tyrant will be rescued; for I will contend with the one who contends with you, and I will save your sons." I praise You that I can count on You to do this in our spiritual warfare, and that through You we shall do valiantly, for You will trample down our enemies.

Isaiah 49:23-25; Psalm 108:13

Your Great Power

*L*ord, I extol You for Your great power toward us who believe— Your tremendous, invincible power that works in us and for us...the same almighty strength You used when You raised Jesus from the dead and seated Him far above all other powers, visible and invisible. You are able to do infinitely beyond all our highest prayers or thoughts. Nothing is impossible with You!

Ephesians 1:19-20; 3:20; Luke 1:37

Thank You that when I praise You and bring my requests to You in simple faith, I plug into Your almighty power...that when I offer a sacrifice of thanksgiving, I open a door for You to rescue me and bless my life, and I prepare the way for You to rescue and bless other people, near and far.

Psalm 50:23 NIV

"So great is your power that your enemies cringe before you." I lift my praise to You, for "no human imagination can take in the startling, revolutionary power, softly, subtly, but with irresistible sweep, that flows down from the crowned Christ among grateful men and women...that flows through the lives of individuals wholly under the gracious influence of the Holy Spirit...through people who simply live in full-faced touch with Christ, and who take that power as the need arises and the sovereign Holy Spirit leads" (adapted from S. D. Gordon). Thank You that I am part of a vast army of people around the world—people who live in full-faced touch with Your Son and move Your mighty hand to bring about Your gracious purposes. Thank You that our influence and our victories are not by human might or power but by Your Spirit.

Psalm 66:3 NIV; Zechariah 4:6

Confident Access

I exult in the free, confident access You have provided so that I can come into Your Presence for warm fellowship, for refreshment, for mercy when I've failed, for grace when I'm in need. What a joy to know that I can draw near to You at any moment, wherever I may be…that I can come boldly to Your throne of grace, assured of Your glad welcome—not because I'm worthy or because I've served You, but because You're a God of grace, a God of unmerited, unlimited favor—not little dribbles of favor reluctantly measured out, but overflowing, superabundant favor. I'm so glad that You welcome me just as I am, simply because Jesus is my risen Savior, and I am alive with His life and righteous with His righteousness!

Ephesians 3:12; Hebrews 10:19-22; 4:16; Ephesians 3:12 TLB; Romans 5:17

Thank You that I can praise and adore You and offer my requests in detail, with thanksgiving…that I can pour out my heart before You, being honest with You about my feelings and my mistakes and my sins. Thank You that when I turn to You as my Lord and confess my sins rather than hiding them or clinging to them, Your forgiveness is immediate and total…that I never need to fear that You will judge or condemn me.

Philippians 4:6; Psalm 62:8; 1 John 1:8-10; Proverbs 28:13

Thank You that I can "be still" (cease striving, let go, relax) and know that You are God…that You are in control…and that I can restfully depend upon You and absorb Your strength and joy and peace. To think that You not only permit me to come before You but You actually desire my fellowship, my worship, my prayers, and my eternal presence! Your desire is for me. "That You should allow Your creature to have fellowship with You is wonderful enough; but that You can desire it, that it gives You satisfaction and joy and pleasure, is almost too much for my understanding."* Thank You.

Psalm 46:10; Isaiah 40:31; John 4:23; Song of Solomon 2:14; 7:10

---

* InterVarsity Staff, *The Quiet Time* (Downers Grove, IL: InterVarsity Press, 1945), 4.

Yielding

*T*hank You that Christ is my Life…that I am a member of His body and a dwelling place of His Spirit. How privileged I am to be indwelt by Your glorious presence (by the whole Trinity: Father, Son, and Holy Spirit!) so that You can display Your excellence to those around me.

Colossians 3:4; 1 Corinthians 12:13; 6:19; Ephesians 3:16-19; 1 Peter 2:9

Thank You for the day when I let go of the whole burden of my sins and rested on the atoning work of Christ—on the total payment He made for me on the cross. And thank You that today, in that same simple way, I can let go of the whole burden of my life and service…of my marriage, children, and all my relationships (past, present, and future), of my inadequacies and my self-dependence, and rest on Your presence working in me through the Holy Spirit. How good it is to transfer these burdens from my shoulders to Yours and to rest on You to work in me and for me and through me! I praise You for the gracious way You infuse me with inner strength through Christ…and so I'm ready for anything You want me to do, and I'm equal to anything You allow to happen in my life.

Isaiah 53:6; Matthew 11:28-29; Psalms 55:22; 68:19; Hebrews 13:20-21; Philippians 4:13

Thank You that I can give myself up to be led by You…that I can go forth praising and at rest, letting You manage me and my day…that I can joyfully depend on You throughout the day, expecting You to guide, to enlighten, to reprove, to teach, to use, and to do in me and with me what You desire…that I can count upon Your working in me and through me as a fact, totally apart from sight or feeling…that I can go forth praising and at rest, believing You and obeying You and ceasing from the burden of trying to manage myself without Your wisdom and power (adapted from Dr. John Hubbard).

Proverbs 3:5-6; Hebrews 13:20-21; Galatians 2:20

Thank You that I can throw the whole weight of my anxieties on You, for I am Your personal concern.

1 Peter 5:7 Phillips

Shining Light

I worship You, Lord of heaven and earth, the God who made the world and all things in it! I extol You for the immensity of Your love in sending Jesus Christ, the long-awaited Messiah, the Savior who died for us, and for all people everywhere. I exalt You because Your plan embraces the whole world and all of time…not just the Middle East, which cradled the gospel, but also Europe and North America, Asia and Africa, the entire Southern Hemisphere, and every tiny island on the globe. Thank You that Jesus, with His blood, purchased sons and daughters for You from every tribe and language and people and nation…and that You yearn for all people everywhere to repent; You have no desire that any person should spend eternity without You!

Acts 17:24; John 3:16; Galatians 4:5-6; 1 John 2:2; Acts 13:47; Revelation 5:9; 2 Peter 3:9

Thank You that You made Your light shine in my heart to give the light of the knowledge of Your glory in the face of Your Son…that You drew me to Yourself and honored me, making me a member of Your royal family and a citizen of Your kingdom…and that You have enlisted me in Your worldwide task force to be Your witness. What a high privilege, that You have destined me to have a share not only in Your love but also in Your glorious purposes, both near and far…that You have gifted me for a unique part in Your global search for people who will repent and believe and learn to live for Your glory. I celebrate my high calling of knowing You and making You known! And I praise You for giving me Your Holy Spirit to fill and empower me, and for promising to be with me always.

2 Corinthians 4:6; Ephesians 2:19; Romans 12:4-6; Acts 1:8; Matthew 28:18-20

"Be exalted, O God, above the heavens; let your glory be over all the earth."

Psalm 57:11 NIV

Finishing What You Began

I exult before You because You are eternal and never changing in Your truth, in Your attributes, and in Your attitude toward me and all Your loved ones. I'm so glad that Your persistent tenderness binds my heart to You forever…that You who began a good work in me will carry it to completion until the day of Christ Jesus. You are utterly faithful and will not abandon the work You have begun.

Psalm 102:25-27; Hebrews 13:8; Jeremiah 31:3; Philippians 1:6; 1 Thessalonians 5:24 Phillips

Thank You for giving us priceless promises, great beyond measure—promises that apply to Your work in me, in my loved ones, in my situation, in my service, and in the whole world…and not one single word of Your good promises has ever failed. I glorify You because no human problem, however hopeless or impossible, is too hard for You. You are able to give life to the dead and call into being that which does not exist. So I need not stagger at Your promises or waver in unbelief. What You have promised You are able to perform!

2 Peter 1:4; 1 Kings 8:56; Jeremiah 32:17,27; Romans 4:17-21

"To You who are able to keep us from falling and to present us before Your glorious presence without fault and with great joy—to the only God our Savior be glory, majesty, power and authority, through Jesus Christ our Lord, before all ages, now and forevermore! Amen."

Jude 24-25 NIV personalized

Praising God...as He Shows Me Myself

A Crucial Question

*H*ow I rejoice, Lord, that the answer to my question "Who am I?" is known so fully and intimately by You, my loving Creator and Father!

I praise You that in the Bible You give me a new self-image, a new sense of identity. Your work of changing me is not primarily directed to the outer margins of my life but to the very center. Through Your Word and Your Holy Spirit, You transform me by renewing my mind.

Romans 12:2

Thank You that Your truth sets us free from pride, insecurity, and other inhibiting negatives. This means I can become the unique person You designed me to be before my birth, when in the womb I was intricately embroidered with great skill.

Psalm 139:14-15 paraphrased

In revealing Your truth to us, thank You for teaching us to acknowledge the negatives about ourselves. From Your point of view, everything we are in the flesh—even our self-attained righteousness—is corrupt. And You cause us to face another fact, one that is negative only from the viewpoint of human pride: our helplessness and inability, on our own, to achieve anything of value in Your sight.

But You don't stop with telling us about the negatives. You teach us to dwell in the positive facts of who we are in Christ now and forever. Yes, we're to glance at the negatives, but we're to *focus* on the positives. This keeps us from wallowing in the weakness and sinfulness of our flesh. Allow me then to "go on…advancing steadily toward the completeness and perfection that belongs to spiritual maturity."

Hebrews 6:1 AMP

I praise You for wanting us to freely acknowledge our dependence on You as we seek to discover who we are on the highest plane possible. I rejoice to realize how You have "brought us into this place of highest privilege where we now stand, and we confidently and joyfully look forward to actually becoming all that God has had in mind for us to be."

Romans 5:2 TLB

Thank You that we can gain an accurate sense of identity as we're securely grounded in You and Your Word. You support us with the confidence that, in Christ, each of us is "all right" as a person forever. Why? Because we share Your belongingness, Your worthiness, Your competence. And the closer I walk with You, the more vividly I'll learn to recognize both the negatives and the positives about myself. As I repeatedly acknowledge the negatives, then turn from them to believe the positives, my daily experience of who I am in Christ expands. By my faith—by trusting the Holy Spirit to work within me—the facts about my identity in You become active forces in my life. And I strengthen my faith by practice—by accepting the truths You reveal and praising You for them.

So I look to You, my gracious Lord, to continue revealing to me who I am as You see fit, according to Your sovereign will. You know fully what I need to understand about myself. You know the distorted ideas and wrong labels in my self-identity that need to be corrected. Help me see these clearly.

Work in me, Lord, so I will love and worship You more and serve You better by choosing a more accurate self-image. Transform me day by day through a fresh new awareness of who You are and who I am in Your sight.

I ask this in Jesus's name, with deep gratefulness for His sacrifice that has won me an intimate relationship with You. I'm so thankful that I can bring my requests to You and freely receive Your answers. Thank You!

My Best Mirror

*F*ather, thank You that to truly see myself, I don't have to look into the mirror of other people's opinions and their approval of my appearance, my performance, and my status. Instead I have the ideal mirror, the mirror of Your love and truth as You have revealed them in Your Word. I can open my Bible and find on its pages accurate insights into how You view me. It shows me Your total forgiveness, Your perfect and limitless love for me, Your constant supply of strength and encouragement, and Your exciting purposes for my life. And these truths never change!

Thank You for telling me in Your Word to direct my thoughts to "whatever is true, whatever is honorable, whatever is just, whatever is pure, whatever is lovely, whatever is commendable." It's in Your Word that I find reliable and uplifting truths, and dwelling on them can produce obedient, confident, and joyful living.

Philippians 4:8 ESV

In Your Word I can see "how very much our Father loves us, for he calls us his children, and that is what we are!" Because of this love, I'm clean through Christ's death on the cross. I'm free from the dominion of sin through His resurrected life. I'm competent to face all of life through His Spirit in me. I'm not expected to be a finished product now, but someday I will be. My destiny is to share in Christ's love, in His purposes, and in His glory now and forever!

1 John 3:1 NLT

What great stability these truths make possible for me! In reality, however, my life is often shaky and faltering. Sometimes I cower before our spiritual enemy. At times I feel discouraged and condemned; I feel I'm in a deep hole and must somehow get myself out before any spiritual progress is possible. Why do I feel this way? Because I base my self-image on (1) Satan's lies, (2) my own past experience, or (3) my feelings—instead of on the solid, glorious, scriptural *facts* of who You are, what You have accomplished, and who I am in You.

I love You, Father, for You give me opportunity to obey Your command to remold my mind from within. In the Bible, You have graciously communicated the keys to help inaugurate a new era in my life—an era of inner strength and serenity as I face life in an insecure world. Your truths about me give me a stable sense of "being somebody"—a solid inner platform of emotional security. From this platform I can live more effectively and confidently in every situation I face. Your truths provide on-the-spot strength to become more like You in my daily life and relationships.

Romans 12:2 Phillips

I offer You the following prayers from Psalm 119 and ask You to be my Counselor as I look into Your Word to discover all You say about who I truly am:

"You made me; you created me. Now give me the sense to follow your commands.... Open my eyes to see the wonderful truths in your instructions."

Psalm 119:73,18 NLT

"O LORD, your unfailing love fills the earth; teach me your decrees.... Teach me your decrees, O LORD; I will keep them to the end.... I will delight in your decrees and not forget your word."

Psalm 119:64,33,16 NLT

"I rejoice in your word like one who discovers a great treasure.... The teaching of your word gives light, so even the simple can understand.... Your word is a lamp to guide my feet and a light for my path."

Psalm 119:162,130,105 NLT

"Let praise flow from my lips, for you have taught me your decrees."

Psalm 119:171 NLT

Father, I am grateful that You are so qualified to teach me as I seek to embrace and live out my true and deepest identity!

I Can Become More

*T*hank You, my Creator, for holding out to me the promise that I can become more than I now am—that I can become more mature, that I can expand my capacity to love and serve You and others. How grateful I am to You for giving me this wonderful opportunity!

You express this promise so clearly to all who are in Christ. You say that as we're "beholding the glory of the Lord," we are all "being transformed" into Christ's image "from one degree of glory to another. For this comes from the Lord who is the Spirit."

2 Corinthians 3:18 ESV

You make it possible for us to "grow up in every way into him who is the head, into Christ," and to "walk in a manner worthy of the Lord, fully pleasing to him, bearing fruit in every good work and increasing in the knowledge of God."

Ephesians 4:15 ESV; Colossians 1:10 ESV

And because You make such maturity and progress possible for each of Your children, You clearly instruct us to "grow in the grace and knowledge of our Lord and Savior Jesus Christ."

2 Peter 3:18 ESV

My heart rejoices that, in You, I *can* begin a process of significant growth no matter where I am in life or where I've been. I *can* take responsibility for moving forward. I praise You for loving me enough to entrust me with this privilege.

Thank You, Lord, for holding out to me this hope. And thank You for Your commitment to sustain me in this process. I'm grateful for the help and strength I can count on through Your Holy Spirit, who is at work in my heart and mind. And through Your Word I hear You say, "Fear not, for I am with you; be not dismayed, for I am your God; I will strengthen you, I will help you, I will uphold you with my righteous right hand."

Isaiah 41:10 ESV

Thank You for making it possible to forget any negative images from my past that can hinder my spiritual and personal growth. Thank You that although I can't entirely erase the old, negative images in my memory, I can overpower them with something better. By deliberate choices I can implant positive and realistic images that are in line with what You say about us. You make it possible for me to say and experience what Paul did: "I focus on this one thing: Forgetting the past and looking forward to what lies ahead, I press on to reach the end of the race and receive the heavenly prize for which God, through Christ Jesus, is calling us."

Philippians 3:13-14 NLT

Keep me on this path, Lord, so that in the days and months and years ahead I may truly please You more and enjoy You in fresh ways.

Mighty God, I look to You and Your power to accomplish these things in me. "You are my strength and my shield; my heart trusts in You, and I am helped."

Psalm 28:7 NIV personalized

Thank You especially for the rich truths about myself that You've inscribed in the pages of the Bible. How amazed I am that these ancient words can be so personally on target in describing me and helping me.

Created by You

*F*ather, wise Creator, I marvel that simply because I am a human being created by You, I have capacities and potential abilities that can lead to a rich life of expansiveness and dignity.

Thank You that I have the ability

...to know who I am and become more than I am.

...to think, to reason, to ponder, to grasp the meaning of reality, and to plan.

...to design and create such things as material objects, art, ideas.

...to love and thereby alleviate suffering and encourage the unfolding of the powers of other people.

Most significantly, I thank You that I have a spirit—an inherent kinship with You, who are Spirit, a potential for personally relating to You. By giving me a spirit, You have designed me with the capacity to delight in Your presence and taste Your reality in the core of my being. I'm a valued person with whom You long for loving involvement, not primarily for what I can do, but simply for who I am. As a unique person, I can bring You pleasure in unique ways.

I'm so grateful, Lord, that this potential spiritual capacity has become reality through a living relationship with You. You have given me spiritual life through a new birth when I chose to trust Christ as my Savior. You have given me this "higher, spiritual life in the eternal kingdom of God."

Mark 8:35 AMP

Thank You for showing me that this living, loving relationship doesn't develop automatically. A satisfying love relationship with You, as with anyone, demands time and teamwork. It must be cultivated, often at the cost of eliminating seemingly important personal interests that are of lesser value. This requires more than a casual, lukewarm, haphazard approach to You.

So I thank You that I can choose to behold You in the Scriptures, letting Your love for me permeate my inner being, breaking down my defenses, and drawing out my warm response. Just as I have known a delightful awe flooding my heart when I see a brilliant sunset, so my love for You rises back to You when I take time to see what You are like and to let You love me.

Father, I desire to strengthen my loving relationship with You. Therefore I pray the following words:

> O God, I have tasted Thy goodness, and it has both satisfied me
> and made me thirsty for more. I am painfully conscious of my
> need of further grace. I am ashamed of my lack of desire.
> O God, the Triune God, I want to want Thee; I long to be
> filled with longing; I thirst to be made more thirsty still. Show me
> Thy glory, I pray Thee, so that I may know Thee indeed. Begin in
> mercy a new work of love within me. Say to my soul, "Rise up,
> my love, my fair one, and come away." Then give me grace to rise
> and follow Thee up from this misty lowland where I have wandered so long. (A. W. Tozer, *The Pursuit of God*)

Thank You, gracious Father, for Your desire and ability and willingness to fill my longing, to quench my thirst, and to begin a new work of love within me.

Made for You and for Love

*Y*ou created me for Yourself! Thank You, Father, for this astonishing truth that encompasses my life's full purpose and significance and worth.

Unfold this truth to me more and more so I can recognize more fully the meaning and guidance it gives to me in the everyday circumstances of my life. I especially give You thanks for relentlessly pursuing my heart and for sparing absolutely no cost in this pursuit. In Jesus, Your Son, You have courted me and won me. I am Yours, and You are mine!

I acknowledge—with amazement—that You desire my love in response. You invite me to love You with all my heart and all my soul and all my mind and all my strength. I pray that more and more You will inspire me and enable me to do this, for You, my loving God, are infinitely worthy of such a response! Help me to grow day by day in offering You my love more fully, and may I grieve or disappoint You less and less.

Today may I gratefully receive and enjoy what You are to me and live more worthily of Your love. Keep taking me to higher levels of knowing You and bringing joy to Your heart.

I'm so glad for this truth that A. W. Tozer brings to our attention: "Every soul is a vast reservoir from which God could receive eternal pleasure." Thank You that this is true of *my* soul. I delight You when I thankfully receive and enjoy all that You are to me, when I consent to increased intimacy and involvement with You. I exult in the truth that I have the inner resource of Your presence and love and power so I can "live in a way worthy of the Lord and to His entire satisfaction."

Colossians 1:10 MLB

Thank You for the fact that developing my relationship with You will increase my ability both to love people and to be loved by them—to unmask myself and open myself to closer relationships. It will also release me to become more than I am—to make my unique contribution, to exercise my special creative abilities, and to enjoy life on a new level.

Your Point of View

Thank You, Lord, for Your unspeakable grace and mercy in helping me more and more to see myself from Your point of view.

Dear Lord, I live in a fallen world where each of us, during at least part of our life, has been separated from You, our true source of identity. Often we have compensated for this with fictions about ourselves that make us feel valuable and important—or at least less left out. Thank You that You are faithfully at work to expose those negative fictions and replace them with positive truths!

How glad I am, Lord, that in doing this, Your purpose is not that I should end up with a low, negative view of who I am. You rip away my unrealistic sense of importance or lack of importance in order to fill me with a sense of value and significance that's grounded in reality. With Your left hand, You take away my phony, inflated or deflated, temporal self-image…and with Your right hand, You give me back a true and eternal and uplifting knowledge of who I am.

Thank You for Your desire to ground our inner beings in reality. I ask You to do this more and more in my life. "Search me, O God, and know my heart! Try me and know my thoughts! And see if there be any grievous way in me, and lead me in the way everlasting!"

Psalm 139:23-24 ESV

I praise You for Your ability to see right through the masks we wear. Your view of us isn't hindered by any of our pretenses. You know all about people in general and each of us in particular. You see the whole package—negative as well as positive—and yet You accept us unreservedly if we belong to Christ.

Humility

I worship You, mighty God, for Your greatness.

I freely acknowledge before You, my Creator, these humbling facts about myself. While You are infinite in capacity and power, I am strictly and severely limited. I'm infinitely less than You; compared to You, I'm tiny in size, in importance, and in influence. With David I can say, "When I look at the night sky and see the work of your fingers —the moon and the stars you set in place—what are mere mortals that you should think about them, human beings that you should care for them?"

Psalm 8:3-4 NLT

You are eternally existent—"from everlasting to everlasting, You are God"—while I am a breath, a passing "vapor that appears for a little while and then vanishes away." So I can learn to pray with David, "My whole lifetime is but a moment to you."

Psalm 90:2 NKJV; James 4:14; Psalm 39:5 TLB

You are Lord and Possessor of all—and there's nothing I can keep or hold or even touch that isn't a gift from You. I receive everything from You. This is true regardless of whether I'm conscious of it—and I need frequent reminders. As Paul asked the Corinthians, "What do you have that God hasn't given you?" I extol You for the truth that Paul told the philosophers of Athens—that it is You who "gives to all mankind life and breath and everything," for it is in You that "we live and move and have our being."

1 Corinthians 4:7 NLT; Acts 17:25,28 ESV

You are fully in control of the universe and everything in it, of every detail, from the celestial sweep of galaxies to the slightest movement of the smallest subatomic particles. "Yours is the dominion, O LORD, and You exalt Yourself as head over all…. You rule over all, and in Your hand is power and might." Therefore there's no choice I can make, no action I can take, that isn't subject to Your physical and moral laws and principles as well as Your sovereign will. When I do my own thing, sooner or later I'm the loser. It doesn't pay to disobey!

1 Chronicles 29:11-12

And I acknowledge before You that all this is not only the way things are…but the way they should be!

So I thank You that I'm accountable to You—responsible for my choices and behavior. For You "will judge us for everything we do, including every secret thing, whether good or bad."

Ecclesiastes 12:14 NLT

I acknowledge how much I need Your guidance. "I know, LORD, that our lives are not our own. We are not able to plan our own course."

Jeremiah 10:23 NLT

I praise You that You designed me to live totally by Your enabling. "Not that we are sufficient of ourselves…our sufficiency is from God."

2 Corinthians 3:5 NKJV

I confess that apart from You, my activities in life are ultimately empty of significance. Apart from You, "everything going on under the sun...is all meaningless—like chasing the wind."

Ecclesiastes 1:14 NLT

And finally, I acknowledge before You this important fact: I'm a member of a fallen humanity—guilty and flawed. As the prophet Isaiah confessed, "All we like sheep have gone astray; we have turned, every one, to his own way."

Isaiah 53:6 NKJV

How well the words of C. S. Lewis sum up my situation and the condition of us all: "Our whole being by its very nature is one vast need; incomplete, preparatory, empty yet cluttered, crying out for Him who can untie things that are now knotted together and tie up things that are still dangling loose." Father, I praise You for Your ability to meet and supply this vast neediness of mine—and I thank You for Your proven willingness to do so.

Significance

*L*oving Father, You give me so many reasons for deep gratitude and appreciation for who I really am!

Thank You that I'm Your special creation—unique and wonderful, personally designed by Your skilled artistry and skillfully put together. "Your hands have made and fashioned me.... I praise you, for I am fearfully and wonderfully made." I am a unique entity that will never be duplicated, and I was never meant to be exactly like anyone else. Thank You for the freedom this gives me to avoid the trap of constantly comparing myself with others.

Psalms 119:73 ESV; 139:14 ESV

Thank You for the high honor and exalted responsibility that You've given to the entire human race. And thank You for making me a member of it. With David I confess how You've made human beings "only a little lower than God and crowned them with glory and honor. You gave them charge of everything you made, putting all things under their authority."

Psalm 8:5-6 NLT

Thank You for sharing something of Yourself in how You've created me. Thank You for creating all human beings in Your image and Your likeness and for crowning us with glory and honor. It is You who made us, and we are Yours. "O LORD, you are our Father; we are the clay, and you are our potter; we are all the work of your hand."

Genesis 1:26-27; Psalms 8:5; 100:3; Isaiah 64:8 ESV

I praise You, Father, that in You "we live and move and have our being."

Acts 17:28 ESV

Most of all, I thank You for demonstrating Your love through Jesus, my beloved Savior. How grateful I am for all that He said and all that He accomplished by living on earth and dying and rising from the dead. I praise and worship You for loving me so deeply. I worship and praise You for demonstrating Your own love for us in this: "While we were still sinners, Christ died for us."

Romans 5:8 NIV

Thank You that Your love for me through Christ also shows that I'm sought-after by You. You say to each of us who will listen, "I have loved you with an everlasting love; therefore with lovingkindness I have drawn you."

Jeremiah 31:3 NKJV

I'm so grateful that Your active seeking for us and drawing us near to Yourself never ceases: "For the eyes of the LORD move to and fro throughout the earth that He may strongly support those whose heart is completely His."

2 Chronicles 16:9

I'm so grateful that, through my salvation in Christ, I discover that I have been created for a high calling and for highly important purposes. There's an eternal reason for my existence, a reason that's extremely important to Christ, for as Paul says of Him, "All things were created through Him and for Him." It's in Christ that each of us is able to fulfill God's words about us through the prophet Isaiah, when You speak of "my sons...and my daughters" and of "everyone who is called by my name, whom I created for my glory, whom I formed and made." My reason for living is wrapped up in Your loving heart, mighty God!

Colossians 1:16 NKJV; Isaiah 43:6-7 NIV

Thank You that the discovery and experience of this high calling is inseparably linked with my relationship with Jesus Christ—a relationship that You designed, for You are the One who invited me into partnership and fellowship with Your Son, Jesus Christ our Lord. Your Word says that each of us is "invited...into partnership with his Son, Jesus Christ our Lord."

1 Corinthians 1:9 NLT

My Flesh

*H*oly God, I acknowledge before You the sinfulness of my natural self, my "flesh." I admit to You the same thing Paul admitted: In my flesh, "nothing good dwells."

Romans 7:18

This fact isn't pleasant, but I choose to accept it. Help me to keep on accepting it and to cast off any remaining illusions that my self-centered, sinful nature can ever be acceptable to You or useful to me. Thank You that truly understanding and acknowledging what we're like in the flesh can humble me and thus open me to the inflow of Your enabling grace.

I acknowledge before You that I want no part in living by this sinful nature and being controlled by it. I recognize the wonderful and exciting truth that my sinful nature is now merely my false self; it's my former self parading as my true self and professing to have my best interests at heart. But my true self is the "new person altogether" that I am in Christ—united with Him, alive with His life, given a position of favor with the living God—cleansed, enriched, and enabled to please and glorify our risen Lord. Having been born of You, I have both a new nature and a new heredity.

2 Corinthians 5:17 Phillips

I acknowledge that the sin that is still present in my flesh doesn't lose its ugliness as I grow spiritually. In spite of all the grace, insight, and power

I enjoy in Christ, I still operate in the flesh if I stop relying on Christ or start believing that my way is better than His. So I rejoice in the fact that, through Christ's death, my sinful side has lost its enslaving hold over me. "Our old sinful selves were crucified with Christ so that sin might lose its power in our lives. We are no longer slaves to sin."

Romans 6:6 NLT

Thank You for breaking my bondage to my sinful nature through the death of Your only Son whom You love so deeply—Jesus Christ, my Savior. How grateful I am that although sin has not been eradicated from my personality, as a believer in Christ, I now share in my innermost being the nature and righteousness of Christ. Thank You that my sinful self has been crucified with Him. Let me not for a single day forget this glorious truth or fail to be grateful to You for it.

Thank You for letting us know in Your Word that You will never improve or remake our old self, our "flesh." Instead You declare it dead and separated from You, and You treat it as such. You have no dealings with it—and You ask us to do the same. For it is "corrupted by lust and deception." It's characterized by a heart that is hopeless, with "nothing to look forward to and no God to whom [it] could turn." It's marked by a mind that is "closed" and "full of darkness." And it is alienated, "cut off from the life of God through…deliberate ignorance of mind and sheer hardness of heart," a separation that leads to "spiritual apathy" and "unbridled sensuality."

Ephesians 4:22 NLT; 2:12 Phillips; 4:18 NLT; 4:18 Phillips; 4:19 AMP

Therefore You tell us to "fling off the dirty clothes of the old way of living, which were rotted through and through with lust's illusions"; then we can "put on the clean fresh clothes of the new life which was made by God's design."

Ephesians 4:22-24 Phillips

Thank You for communicating in Your Word that I can dispel the darkness of my sinful nature not by trying to push it out of my personality but by letting in light—Your faithful and powerful light.

Thank You, Lord, that I can face the existence of my sinful nature with the breathtaking knowledge that I am a new person in Christ Jesus. "The old has passed away; behold, the new has come." I leave the old behind and run forward, eager to enjoy all the newness and fullness You have for me!

2 Corinthians 5:17 ESV

Adventure in Christ

*F*ather, I'm so glad that against the dark backdrop of the negative facts about us—what we're like in our sinful flesh—You paint a beautiful portrait of who we are *in Christ*. Thank You that who I am in Christ is what matters most, both now and forever.

I celebrate that I never again need to rely on my appearance, my performance, or my status to define who I am. I think of my physical appearance as simply a picture frame in which I can display Your love and sufficiency. My performance becomes simply an expression of who I really am in Christ rather than an attempt to gain support for my self-image. And my status is important only as it gives me opportunity to glorify You and serve others; it does not indicate who I am.

Thank You that through my oneness with Christ my actions become a way of giving love rather than trying to earn an ego-building response from other people. I no longer need to depend on how people respond to me, and I escape from evaluating myself in the mirror of human approval.

In praise and worship, I acknowledge that every truth about me is rooted in who *You* are—Your attributes, attitudes, and actions. Because You are love, I am loved. Because You're the Redeemer who shed Your blood for us, I am ransomed. Because You're the Giver, I can be a receiver. Because You desire me, I am both desirable and desired. Because You have chosen me, I am intimately related to the Supreme Ruler of all. The portrait You have revealed of Yourself undergirds Your portrait of who I am in Christ.

How grateful I am for all that this means for me. For every need or problem I face, there's always a corresponding truth (or truths) about You that can see me through triumphantly, with calm trust in You.

Thank You again that I can keep returning to our most complete revelation of You—Your written Word—to keep learning more about You. You are revealed in everything the Scriptures record—the commandments, history, poetry, prophecy, promises. All of it reveals Your personality, Your ways, Your standards and plans and gracious purposes, and Your heart for each of us.

Father, I invite You to lovingly invade all my thinking about myself. Expose further ways in which I'm holding on to what is deceptive and inadequate, and encourage me to cling to the exciting truths You have revealed—truths that confirm who I really am in Your sight. For You "revive and stimulate me according to Your word!"

Psalm 119:25 AMP

I praise You for how faithful You are to enlighten me, to deliver me, and to support me. Thank You for teaching me to yield more fully to You and obey You more constantly. Guide me in the adventure of full reliance on You. I trust You to transform me and empower me, enabling me to fulfill all You have in mind for me to be and to do.

My Need

*T*hank You, Lord, that when You let me hunger psychologically or emotionally or spiritually—then meet that heightened need with Yourself—it helps me understand how perfectly You provide for me.

Thank You for our assurance in the Scriptures of Your attention to help the needy: "For the LORD hears the needy and does not despise his own people." "He stands beside the needy, ready to save them." "God blesses those who are poor and realize their need for him, for the Kingdom of Heaven is theirs."

Psalms 69:33 ESV; 109:31 NLT; Matthew 5:3 NLT

I praise You that whenever my longing and sense of need become like an intense thirst, I can find help in remembering what You are like: "When the poor and needy seek water, and there is none, and their tongue is parched with thirst, I the LORD will answer them; I the God of Israel will not forsake them. I will open rivers on the bare heights, and fountains in the midst of the valleys. I will make the wilderness a pool of water, and the dry land springs of water."

Isaiah 41:17-18 ESV

As I recognize what You are like, I can freely admit how needy I am. I can acknowledge with David, "I am poor and needy, and my heart is wounded within me." In my shortcomings I can know the same truth

David knew: "As for me, I am poor and needy, but the Lord takes thought for me." The King of kings is thinking about me!

Psalms 109:22 NIV; 40:17 ESV

So I can ask You earnestly, with confidence, "Do not withhold Your tender mercies from me, O LORD; let Your lovingkindness and Your truth continually preserve me.... Be pleased, O LORD, to deliver me; O LORD, make haste to help me!"

Psalm 40:11,13 NKJV

And as I see with greater clarity the truth about myself, it elevates You to first place in my heart and life. You enable me to tell You even this: "I desire you more than anything on earth." "I have Thee as my very own in the land of the living."

Psalms 73:25 NLT; 142:5 Moffatt

Thank You that the more I see You responding to my needs, the more I'll be able to affirm with David, "My soul finds rest in God alone; my salvation comes from him. He alone is my rock and my salvation; he is my fortress, I will never be shaken."

Psalm 62:1-2 NIV

I'm so grateful, Lord, that I don't have to try to hide my needs. I can always openly confess them before You as part of my ongoing relationship with You.

I thank You that You meet me where I am and that You are at work in me to make me more than I am. So I choose to thank You for Your gracious attitude toward the ways I fall short. What a comfort to know that You fully understand my feelings of weakness and inadequacy.

In the following specific ways, I acknowledge that I am poor, needy, weak, and dependent:

Called and Chosen

*T*hank You that I've been called personally *by* You and *to* You. I know this calling is personal because You use my name. To each of Your children You say, "I have called you by your name; you are Mine." Thank You for making Your Son my Good Shepherd who calls me by name.

Isaiah 43:1 NKJV; John 10:3

My heart rejoices in You, Lord, for the amazing privilege of being chosen by You in eternity past. I acknowledge Your truth that my calling is actually older than I am. In Your Word, You teach each of Your servants to acknowledge this: "The LORD called me from the womb, from the body of my mother he named my name." From You I hear the same assurance You gave the prophet Jeremiah: "Before I formed you in the womb I knew you." You have "called us with a holy calling," according to Your "purpose and grace which was given to us in Christ Jesus before time began."

Isaiah 49:1 ESV; Jeremiah 1:5 NKJV; 2 Timothy 1:9 NKJV

I praise You that my eternal calling stretches as far into the future as it does into the past, and it ensures my share in the Lord's glory. "Those whom he predestined he also called, and those whom he called he also justified, and those whom he justified he also glorified."

Romans 8:30 ESV

I celebrate the fact that I've been "called according to Your purpose" and that Your purpose includes not only effective service for You but also an intimate relationship with You. For You tell us, "I have called you...saying, 'You are my servant.'" Everything about Your calling of us is permeated with Your own eternal and changeless character. Your reason for choosing us flows out of Your loving character and Your faithfulness to fulfill Your promises: "The LORD fastened His affection upon you and chose you...because the LORD loved you."

Romans 8:28 ESV personalized; Isaiah 41:9 NLT; Deuteronomy 7:6-8 MLB

Just as with everything else in Your actions and attitudes toward me, Your choice of me is inseparably linked with Your eternal love: "Even before he made the world, God loved us and chose us in Christ to be holy and without fault in his eyes." This everlasting and decisive love is wrapped up with Your sovereign will, "for he chose us in advance, and he makes everything work out according to his plan."

Ephesians 1:4,11 NLT

How wonderful to know that I never need to fear that You will reject me, for to be chosen by You is the opposite of being rejected. You say, "You are My servant," and You remind each of us, "I have chosen you and not rejected you."

Isaiah 41:9

And Lord, I count on You to guide and empower me to lead a life worthy of my holy calling. Thank You again that I'm a chosen one— called to love and obey the King of kings and Lord of lords, the Supreme Ruler of all things.

Desired

I love You, Lord, because You have first loved me. You are my Beloved, and I am Yours, and I rejoice that Your desire is for me. You called and chose us because You *desire* us; Your choice of us arose out of the fervent passion of Your heart.

1 John 4:10; Song of Solomon 7:10

Therefore I rejoice as I hear You say, "Rise up, my love, my fair one, and come away.... O my dove...let me see your face, let me hear your voice; for your voice is sweet, and your face is lovely."

Song of Solomon 2:10,14 NKJV

And though we are "prone to wander," as the old hymn says, Your desire ensures Your active courtship of us as Your bride. You say, "I will allure her, put her alone and apart, and speak to her heart." Your desire for us means I'll never be separated from Your loving notice and concern. I can exclaim, as our brother David did, "Look at how the Eternal marks me out for favor! The Eternal listens when I call to Him." I can join David as he cries out with delight, "How precious are your thoughts about me, O God. They cannot be numbered! I can't even count them; they outnumber the grains of sand!"

Hosea 2:14 Moffatt; Psalms 4:3 Moffatt; 139:17-18 NLT

God of boundless love, thank You for seeing and knowing everything about me. As I rest in the righteousness of Christ, I can count on Your loving attention, for "the eyes of the LORD are on the righteous." You who number the very hairs of my head cannot forget me, for You say, "See, I have engraved you on the palms of my hands."

Psalm 34:15 NKJV; Matthew 10:30; Isaiah 49:16 NIV

I rejoice that Your desire for me never turns cold but that You continue to shower me with Your gifts and blessings. You are always thinking of me, providing for me, guiding me. The Lord of heaven and earth loves to bestow rich gifts on His desired ones, and therefore I can confidently look forward to seeing and experiencing "[all that] God has prepared (made and keeps ready) for those who love Him." Most Beloved One, I rejoice to know that my future is as bright as Your love and promises.

1 Corinthians 2:9 AMP

My heart is thrilled to know that as I approach this One who desires us so intensely, my response triggers "joy in the presence of the angels of God." For I was lost, but now I'm found—just like the missing coin and the stray lamb and the wayward son in the stories Jesus told in Luke 15. I am the returning prodigal swept up in a parent's passionate welcome: "But while he was still a long way off, his father saw him and felt compassion, and ran and embraced him and kissed him." Thank You for running to me in my need and putting Your loving arms around me. For all this and more, I offer You my praise and thanksgiving—and my love!

Luke 15:10 NKJV; 15:20 ESV

No Longer Condemned

*L*ord God, You are mighty to save!

Isaiah 63:1 NKJV

Thank You for delivering me from the condemnation I deserve. Thank You for Your promise of salvation: "The LORD redeems the soul of His servants, and none of those who trust in Him shall be condemned."

Psalm 34:22 NKJV

How I thank You for delivering me from guilt. For in my old identity —my former self—guilt persisted as a prominent feature. My guilt was like a strong glue that bonded me to sin and death. Even when I could faintly glimpse that sin was my enemy and that I was enslaved to it, guilt held me like a vise under sin's rule. The law saw to that. It held me to the penalty I had brought on myself by aligning myself with sin. I stood condemned before You because I was a fallen person—contaminated by sin, unfit for intimacy with You, the Holy One.

Thank You for overcoming the barricades I had erected in my heart against You as I chose to go my own way. In this regard I was like every other human being, just as the apostle Paul says: "We ourselves were thoughtless, disobedient, led astray, slaves to passions and pleasures of all sorts, wasting our time in malice and envy, detestable, and hating one another."

Titus 3:3 MLB

But now I have a guilt-free identity in Christ for one reason alone: "The goodness and loving kindness of God our Savior appeared." How grateful I am for this freedom from guilt that is mine in Your Son, Jesus Christ, the Holy One. Thank You that You "made Him who knew no sin to be sin on our behalf, so that we might become the righteousness of God in Him." Christ ransomed me for You, and now I'm fully Yours.

Titus 3:4 ESV; 2 Corinthians 5:21

Thank You that Jesus is my advocate, my merciful and faithful High Priest before You, who comes to my aid when I am tempted, providing the way of escape. For "we have an Advocate with the Father, Jesus Christ the righteous; and He Himself is the propitiation for our sins."

Hebrews 8:1; 2:17-18; 1 Corinthians 10:13; 1 John 2:1-2

Now in Christ I can continually savor the fact that through His sacrifice I can joyfully view myself as acquitted. Thank You, my Lord and Savior! I'm no longer condemned! What greater relief and joy can there be for one whose guilt was so real? "Blessed and happy and to be envied are those whose iniquities are forgiven and whose sins are covered up and completely buried. Blessed and happy and to be envied is the person of whose sin the Lord will take no account nor reckon it against him."

Romans 4:7-8 AMP

"So then there is no condemnation at all for those who are in union with Christ Jesus." I thank You, Lord, that for me such condemnation no longer exists. The reason for it is gone, by virtue of what Christ's death achieved: "God crossed out the whole debt against us in His account books. He no longer counted the laws that we had broken. He nailed the account book to the cross and closed the account."

Romans 8:1 Williams; Colossians 2:14 Laubach

Thank You for this firm promise from the lips of the Lord Jesus: "I most solemnly say to you, whoever listens to me and believes Him who has sent me...will never come under condemnation." With joy I hear Your good news: "Do not be afraid, for I have ransomed you."

John 5:24 Williams; Isaiah 43:1 NLT

Thank You again that in Christ You've delivered me from condemnation. "For you love me so much! You are constantly so kind! You have rescued me from deepest hell." Therefore I can say, "My rescue comes from Him alone; rock, rescue, refuge, He is all to me."

Psalms 86:13 TLB; 62:1-2 Moffatt

Clean and More

hank You, Father, that I'm no longer defiled and corrupt. In Christ I'm entirely clean—and through His blood I can "escape the corruption in the world caused by evil desires." You have purified my conscience from its deadly defilement. How I thank You!

2 Peter 1:4 NIV

Thank You that Your cleansing goes so deep and accomplishes so much—for the blood of Christ is able to "purify our conscience from the deeds of death, that we may serve the living God."

Hebrews 9:14 Phillips

Thank You for fulfilling Your promise through Your prophets long ago: "You will be clean; I will cleanse you from all your impurities and from all your idols.... I will save you from all your uncleanness." "Though your sins are like scarlet, I will make them as white as snow. Though they are red like crimson, I will make them as white as wool."

Ezekiel 36:25,29 NIV; Isaiah 1:18 NLT

Now, Lord, with all Your redeemed people I have the privilege of drawing near to You "with a sincere heart in full assurance of faith, having my heart sprinkled to cleanse me from a guilty conscience and having my body washed with pure water."

Hebrews 10:22 NIV personalized

Thank You that You forgive me not simply for my sake but also for Your sake. For You say, "I, I am he who blots out your transgressions for my own sake." In forgiving and removing my sins, You have fulfilled Your ancient promise to Your people: "I will forgive their iniquity, and their sin I will remember no more."

Isaiah 43:25 ESV; Jeremiah 31:34 NKJV

I praise You for Your forgiveness, for it flows from the essence of Your character. "O Lord, you are so good, so ready to forgive, so full of unfailing love for all who ask for your help."

Psalm 86:5 NLT

"There is forgiveness with You...that You may be reverently feared and worshiped." And because the forgiveness that cleanses me has been purchased at the highest price possible—the lifeblood of Christ—it is precious beyond imagining: "In Him we have redemption through His blood, the forgiveness of sins."

Psalm 130:4 AMP; Ephesians 1:7 NKJV

How I thank You that I have been bathed by my new birth—and now I only have to wash my feet by simply confessing when I fail to obey You. Thank You for Your encouragement to quickly and sincerely acknowledge my offenses. Your Word teaches me this: "If we confess our sins, He is to be depended on, since He is just, to forgive us our sins and to cleanse us from every wrong." I can count on You to be like the prodigal son's father—not giving me an additional lecture when I come to You in repentance but calling for a robe and a ring and a feast in my honor!

1 John 1:9 Williams; Luke 15:17-24

I draw near to You this very moment to celebrate the ever-refreshing cleanness You have given me in my inmost being. For my redemption does not merely mean that I'm no longer "wrong" in Your eyes. It also means that I am fully "made right with God through Christ." "We are justified (acquitted, declared righteous, and given a right standing with God) through faith."

2 Corinthians 5:21 NLT; Romans 5:1 AMP

I come to You wearing the clean and shining robe of righteousness, the garments of salvation that You have clothed me with. For being redeemed means not only casting off the ragged, soiled clothing of my sins but also putting on glorious new garments of righteousness. "I will greatly rejoice in the LORD; my soul shall exult in my God, for he has clothed me with the garments of salvation; he has covered me with the robe of righteousness, as a bridegroom decks himself like a priest with a beautiful headdress, and as a bride adorns herself with her jewels." This verse is a beautiful picture to me of what it means to be "justified freely by his grace through the redemption that came by Christ Jesus."

Isaiah 61:10 ESV; Romans 3:24 NIV

Thank You again that as a new person in Christ I am forever clean. And thank You for Your reminder in Your Word that all this calls for my grateful response in how I live and how I approach You: "Since we have these promises...let us purify ourselves from everything that contaminates body and spirit."

2 Corinthians 7:1 NIV

Fully Alive

I give thanks to You, Father, for giving me life—not only physical life, but also spiritual life! You have made me spiritually alive through the resurrection of Christ, who is my life.

Colossians 3:4

Thank You that I can always view myself as "alive to God, alert to him, through Jesus Christ our Lord." You tell me I can now consider myself "as having ended my relation to sin but living in unbroken relation to God" through union with Christ Jesus. In a way that was utterly impossible before, I have become "alive to all that is good."

Romans 6:11 TLB; 6:11 Williams personalized; 1 Peter 2:24 Phillips

I magnify You for the mighty power You displayed when You raised Your Son from the tomb. What an incredible exhibit of Your life-giving power! How I rejoice that my entrance into spiritual aliveness is inseparably linked with Christ's resurrection. "God is so rich in mercy, and he loved us so much, that even though we were dead because of our sins, he gave us life when he raised Christ from the dead." This same life—the resurrected life of Christ—is mine! And by it, in my innermost being, I can live in unbroken union with You just as Your Son, Jesus, does. Thank You, my mighty and loving Father!

Ephesians 2:4-5 NLT

Thank You that at my new birth, a radical, night-and-day change took place in my innermost being—in my true and eternal person. It was a passing out of death into life: "And you He made alive, who were dead in trespasses and sins."

Ephesians 2:1 NKJV

Father, I worship You as "the life-giving God," as "the living Father." I rejoice in the words of aliveness that Jesus used to describe You: "The Father has life in Himself and is self-existent." "The Father raises the dead and gives them life." "He is not the God of the dead, but of the living."

1 Timothy 6:13 MSG; John 6:57 NKJV; 5:26 AMP; 5:21; Luke 20:38 NIV

I worship You as the God "who gives life to the dead and calls into existence the things that do not exist."

Romans 4:17 ESV

I praise You that Your Son, Jesus, is "the Author of life," and I thank You that by believing in Him, I "have already passed from death into life." Thank You for how Christ so closely identifies my life with Himself: "I am the resurrection and the life.... Because I live, you will live also.... The Son also gives life to whom He wishes."

Acts 3:15 ESV; John 5:24 NLT; 11:25; 14:19; 5:21

And thank You for how Christ has imparted this life to me through the wonderful gift of the Holy Spirit, "the Spirit of life," the One who "makes alive." How grateful I am for how He sustains me in this new aliveness, as my constant source of spiritual breath and health and wholeness. For "it is the Spirit who gives life."

Romans 8:2 NKJV; 2 Corinthians 3:6 AMP; John 6:63

Thank You that because I have received "this wildly extravagant life-gift," it's now a vital and daily possibility that "the [resurrection] life of Jesus…may be shown forth by and in our bodies." Rather than living selfishly, I "may [henceforth] live to and for God."

Romans 5:17 MSG; 2 Corinthians 4:10 AMP; Galatians 2:19 AMP

How I praise You for Your love for me in wanting me to experience all that this aliveness means. Thank You for connecting me eternally with the realities of heaven, where Christ sits at Your right hand in honor and power, and for Your desire to have this transform the way I think. Since I "have been raised to new life with Christ," You instruct me to set my "sights on the realities of heaven, where Christ sits in the place of honor at God's right hand." You tell me, "Apply your mind to things above, not to things on earth." Thank You for making this possible!

Colossians 3:1 NLT; 3:2 MLB

Thank You that I can keep coming to the Scriptures and nurturing my mind with the truth I find there. "You have the words of eternal life." Thank You for this promise from Jesus: "Whoever continues to feed on Me [whoever takes Me for his food and is nourished by Me] shall [in his turn] live through and because of Me."

John 6:68 NKJV; 6:57 AMP

Thank You for awakening my mind and heart so that I can think about these realities and treasure them and turn from fleshly ways as I depend on Your life in me.

You are the God who "preserves alive all living things." I acknowledge that all of my life—physical and spiritual—is in Your hands and under Your control.

1 Timothy 6:13 AMP

Dead to Sin

*T*hank You that my new life in Christ comes hand in hand with a corresponding death. You say to me, "As far as this world is concerned, you are already dead, and your true life is a hidden one in God, through Christ."

Colossians 3:3 Phillips

Thank You, Lord, for allowing me to become a partaker of Christ's death and all its benefits. Thank You that I've been acquitted from all my guilt, that I have "died to sin." I no longer live under sin's reign.

Romans 6:2 NKJV

Thank You for the share I have in Christ's crucifixion and burial, just as I also share in His resurrection. It's a death and burial so real that it means I have actually been crucified with Your Son, Jesus. I glory in the Cross of Christ, because on that cross He satisfied the righteous demand of Your wrath against me because of my sins.

Romans 6:3-6; Galatians 2:20; 6:14

Thank You that I can continually rely on the facts that I'm both dead to sin and alive to You. Both facts, I know, are humanly impossible. But You, the God of the impossible, have made them realities, and I simply accept them by faith. I take You at Your Word. I'm dead as far as sin is concerned, crucified through Christ's death...but I'm also alive with

Christ's powerful life, alive through His resurrection, and "the God-given life-principle continues to live" inside me. Thank You for how these two truths together cancel out my old relationship with sin and death and inaugurate my new relationship with You. I accept this as fact and depend on it in my daily life as I trust in You.

1 John 3:9 Williams

Father of all life, I praise You as One who cannot lie, and therefore I know that these facts are unquestionably true.

I acknowledge that any flirting with sin is absolutely inconsistent with who I really am—with my true identity in Christ. I acknowledge the truth that there's absolutely nothing about sin that is in any way helpful to my best interests, or even neutral. All sin is my enemy. Therefore when sin tries to masquerade as my true being—when it presses its claim on me and pretends to represent my true interests—I can choose instead to believe Your Word. I can count on the realities about me that You have pronounced. Thank You for making it possible for me to yield to You and obey You in this new way.

How grateful I am for the constant help You provide in my lifelong responsibility of putting to death all that belongs to my sinful nature.

Romans 8:13; Colossians 3:5

Thank You again for ending my relationship to sin through the Cross of Christ. I acknowledge before You that the real me hates sin and is aligned against it. The real me longs for my whole personality to be conformed to the image of Christ.

I praise You for Your holiness, Your hatred of sin. And I thank You for giving me new life so that in the depths of my being I can—with You—share in that hatred. How grateful I am that as I rely on You as my Life, I can do all that You want me to do!

Thank You again that in Christ I'm dead to sin—but alive to You!

Romans 6:11

Filled

*F*ather, although in the flesh I'm proud and self-serving, I accept my position in Christ as a created being in total need of You, glorying in You alone.

In myself I'm empty and incomplete, but in Your Son I'm filled and complete. I'm lacking nothing, because He more than compensates for my lack at every point of need.

I praise You for the love You have lavished upon me. Because of it, my life overflows with Your blessings. You fill and satisfy me. You grant me everything I need. You enflame my heart with joy. "My cup overflows." You say to me, "All things are yours...and you are Christ's, and Christ is God's."

Psalm 23:5 NIV; I Corinthians 3:21,23 ESV

Thank You that in Christ I have a rich and full supply of grace, peace, forgiveness, wisdom, nourishment, strength, light, comfort—all that I need for abundant living, whatever my circumstances may be. You make it possible for me to be "mature in the Lord, measuring up to the full and complete standard of Christ." "Praised be...God...for giving us through Christ every spiritual benefit as citizens of Heaven!" Thank You especially for the gift of Your Holy Spirit, "that we might realize and comprehend and appreciate the gifts [of divine favor and blessing so freely and lavishly] bestowed on us by God."

Ephesians 4:13 NLT; 1:3 Phillips; I Corinthians 2:12 AMP

Thank You especially for the overflowing joy You make possible for me. "In your presence there is fullness of joy." I hold on to the promise of Jesus: "You will be filled with my joy. Yes, your joy will overflow!"

Psalm 16:11 ESV; John 15:11 NLT

I praise You for the fullness of Christ Himself, and I thank You for how this makes possible my own enrichment. For "He was full of unfailing love and faithfulness." In Christ, "the whole fullness of deity dwells bodily, and you have been filled in him, who is the head of all rule and authority." "And from his fullness we have all received, grace upon grace."

John 1:14 NLT; Colossians 2:9-10 ESV; John 1:16 ESV

Thank You that in Christ I can be "filled with all the fullness of God," "filled with the fruit of righteousness that comes through Jesus Christ, to the glory and praise of God," and "filled with the knowledge of his will in all spiritual wisdom and understanding."

Ephesians 3:19 NKJV; Philippians 1:11 ESV; Colossians 1:9 ESV

I praise You for Your ability to extend this fullness to every aspect of my daily life, just as Your Word assures me: "God is able to provide you with every blessing in abundance, so that you may always have enough of everything and may provide in abundance for every good work." I praise and thank You for this truth expressed in Your Word: "God has given us everything we need for living a godly life. We have received all of this by coming to know him, the one who called us to himself by means of his marvelous glory and excellence."

2 Corinthians 9:8 RSV; 2 Peter 1:3 NLT

And thank You for how You want this fullness to overflow in love and praise to You and in love and service to those around me—my brothers and sisters in Christ as well as those who do not yet know You.

Always a Receiver

I praise You, Lord, for how gracious You are—generous beyond imagining! You don't give reluctantly, for You delight to do good to each of Your beloved children.

I praise You as the Giver, the Source of the abundant grace that brings me every spiritual blessing in Christ. "Every good gift and every perfect gift is from above, and comes down from the Father of lights."

James 1:17 NKJV

Thank You that in Christ I stand permanently in Your unmerited favor. "Whatever I am now, it is all because God poured out his special favor on me." I am a receiver of a full and steady overflow that is not limited by my failures, for where sin abounds, grace abounds much more.

1 Corinthians 15:10 NLT; Romans 5:20 NKJV

The abundance of Your grace—Your unmerited favor—makes my heart sing for joy.

You offered me eternal life, now and forever, and I have gladly received it.

You offered me oneness with Your Son through the Holy Spirit, and I have gladly received it.

When I sin, You offer me forgiveness; I gladly receive Your inner cleansing.

In Christ, You offer me love and wisdom and strength, and I gladly receive them.

Day by day You offer me all that I need for life and godliness. I gratefully open myself to receive with thanksgiving all that You provide.

Thank You that as I feed on God's Word, the Holy Spirit enlightens me to grasp these truths and their significance. Thank You for how this enables me to hold my head high—not in pride but in humble gratitude, submission, and dependence. For "I am not worthy of all the unfailing love and faithfulness you have shown to me."

Genesis 32:10 NLT

I give thanks to You, for You are good, and Your steadfast love endures forever.

Psalm 136:1 RSV

New Altogether

hank You, loving Father, for Your gift to me of newness and for enabling me to continually grow in my experience of all that this newness means.

How I praise You that I've been born out of the old and into the new! I've been born into Your family by receiving Your only begotten Son—by believing in Him as my Savior.

Thank You that in Christ I have become "a new person altogether— the past is finished and gone, everything has become fresh and new." For He saved me "through the washing of rebirth and renewal by the Holy Spirit." You make it possible for me to live "a brand new kind of life." "Just as Christ rose from the dead through the Father's glorious power, so we too shall conduct ourselves in a new way of living."

2 Corinthians 5:17 Phillips; Titus 3:5 NIV; Colossians 3:10 TLB; Romans 6:4 MLB

Thank You for fulfilling Your ancient promise: "I will give you a new heart—I will give you new and right desires—and put a new spirit within you." And for giving Your promise about our eternal future: "Behold, I am making all things new."

Ezekiel 36:26 TLB; Revelation 21:5

Thank You for teaching me in Your Word that the moment I die, my spirit and my personality—the new and true me—will immediately go to be "at home with the Lord." I will leave behind all my sinful tendencies, all my old patterns of living. And when Christ returns, He'll give me a new body, totally free from even the slightest remnant of sin and death. My new body will be "imperishable" and "supernatural"; it will be "raised in honor and glory"; and it will be "resurrected in strength and endued with power."

2 Corinthians 5:8 NIV; 1 Corinthians 15:42-44 AMP

And I rejoice in the truth that in my innermost being, as a new creation through Christ's life in me, this has already happened to me spiritually! "The old condition has passed away, a new condition has come." Thank You, Father, for who I am now in spirit…and for what I shall be in totality in my eternal future.

2 Corinthians 5:17 Williams

I thank You again, Father, that in Christ I am new. "The old has gone, the new has come!"

2 Corinthians 5:17 NIV

Empowered

*H*ow I rejoice, Lord, that "in your hand are power and might, and in your hand it is to make great and to give strength to all."

1 Chronicles 29:12 ESV

Almighty God, thank You that through my union with Christ I can experience power and enabling beyond what I have ever known. Thank You that I no longer need to be anxious, for in Christ I am adequate…enabled…empowered. Anxiety and fear are no longer realistic, for in You I have every reason to be confident, trusting, and at rest.

Thank You for Your many promises of strength: "In quietness and confidence shall be your strength." "The joy of the LORD is your strength."

Isaiah 30:15 NKJV; Nehemiah 8:10 NKJV

I praise and thank You for the strength You make available to me. "The LORD is the source of all my righteousness and strength." "My flesh and my heart may fail, but God is the strength of my heart and my portion forever." As I labor in the tasks You assign me, and as I face the suffering You allow, I can look to You and Your grace for enabling. I can say as Paul did, "I exert all my strength in reliance upon the power of Him who is mightily at work within me." In You, I find solid support, even in the most difficult circumstances.

Isaiah 45:24 NLT; Psalm 73:26 NIV; Colossians 1:29 Weymouth

Thank You for Your invitation to actively seek and find my strength in You. You say, "Trust in the Lord God always, for in the Lord Jehovah is your everlasting strength." "Search for the LORD and for his strength; continually seek him."

Isaiah 26:4 TLB; I Chronicles 16:11 NLT

So my heart rejoices in You, the strongest Strong One, as my constant source of energy and strength and protection. "You have been a stronghold to the poor, a stronghold to the needy in his distress."

Isaiah 25:4 ESV

Therefore, through Christ "I have strength for all things...[I am ready for anything and equal to anything...; I am self-sufficient in Christ's sufficiency]."

Philippians 4:13 AMP

Enlightened

I praise You, Lord God, for You are Light, the One in whom there is no darkness at all.

1 John 1:5

I glorify You, for as I follow You, I shall not walk in darkness, because I have the light of life—everlasting light.

John 8:12; Isaiah 60:19

Thank You that Your light gives me a bright new understanding of my life and purpose, for "the path of the righteous is like the light of dawn, which shines brighter and brighter until full day."

Proverbs 4:18 ESV

Thank You for how Your light shines through Your Son, who is Himself the bright radiance, the flawless expression of Your glory. He is the light that has conquered my darkness. He is the light that overcomes my fears. And He makes possible a shining clarity in my thoughts and actions, as I "walk in the Light as He Himself is in the Light." Through His indwelling presence, I go from being "full of darkness" to being "full of light." Thank You that in Christ my eyes have been opened so I could "turn from darkness to light and from the power of Satan to God."

Hebrews 1:3 Phillips; Psalm 27:1; 1 John 1:7; Luke 11:34-36 NKJV; Acts 26:18 ESV

I praise You, Father, that Your spiritual light is like sunshine in my life, warming my inner being and allowing my mind and heart to see what You want me to see. Thank You for the light of Your guidance, shining on my pathway, so I can confidently say, "The LORD is my light and my salvation." "Though I fall, I will rise again. Though I sit in darkness, the LORD will be my light."

Psalm 27:1 NKJV; Micah 7:8 NLT

Thank You especially for the steady streams of light that come through Your Word. "Your word is a lamp to my feet and a light to my path.... The unfolding of your words gives light."

Psalm 119:105,130 ESV

Thank You for Your many bright promises of light for Your people: "I will lead the blind in a way that they do not know, in paths that they have not known I will guide them. I will turn the darkness before them into light." "The LORD will be to you an everlasting light." "The people walking in darkness have seen a great light." "Light dawns in the darkness for the upright."

Isaiah 42:16 ESV; 60:19 NKJV; 9:2 NIV; Psalm 112:4 ESV

I praise You that in You I am enlightened. How grateful I am that You have called me out of darkness into Your marvelous light that I may show forth Your excellencies.

1 Peter 2:9

Belonging

*L*oving Father, thank You for supplying everything I need in my sense of who I am. You supply it as I let You relate to me and as I learn to know You better.

Thank You for wanting me and for bringing me to Yourself for Your own enjoyment and glory. I'm Yours! I belong to the Almighty God of the universe! What a thrill this is—and what a soothing remedy for the times when I'm tempted to feel alienated or excluded or ignored by others. I always have You, and I'll always belong to You.

I praise You for Your rich love that has welcomed me into a union with You, a union that transcends all others in intimacy and permanence. In Your eyes I will never be an outsider but always an insider. In Christ, I never have to view myself as deficient or as inferior to those who see themselves as exclusive or elite. I already belong in the special group that matters most. I qualify simply because Christ is in me.

Colossians 1:27

Now I belong to Christ Jesus, for I have been united with Him. I am Christ's, and Christ is God's. Therefore, through Christ, I belong to God, the ultimate source of belongingness.

Ephesians 2:13 NLT; 1 Corinthians 3:23 ESV

Thank You that "through the shedding of Christ's blood" I am now inside the circle of God's love. Thank You for Your church, which is my eternal family and household and nation. I "belong in God's household with every other Christian." I am a full member of "the church of the firstborn, whose names are written in heaven."

Ephesians 2:13 Phillips; 2:19 TLB; Hebrews 12:23 NIV

Belonging to You means I can embrace with certainty the truth that I really am Your son or daughter. For Jesus is "the firstborn among many brothers and sisters"—and I'm one of them, as someone "born of the Spirit." For "to all who received him, to those who believed in his name, he gave the right to become children of God." "How great is the love the Father has lavished on us, that we should be called children of God! And that is what we are!"

Romans 8:29 NLT; John 3:6 NKJV; 1:12 NIV; 1 John 3:1 NIV

I rest in this assurance that You give us: "I will be a Father to you, and you shall be My sons and daughters, says the LORD Almighty." Thank You for how You keep intensifying my personal experience of Your fatherhood through Your Spirit. For Your Word tells us, "Because you are sons, God has sent the Spirit of His Son into your hearts, crying 'Abba,' that is, 'Father.' So you are no longer a slave, but a son; and if a son, then an heir by God's own act." "For all who are led by the Spirit of God are sons of God."

2 Corinthians 6:18 NKJV; Galatians 4:6-7 Williams; Romans 8:14 ESV

I rejoice in the warm embrace of belongingness that surrounds me—all because of You! By Your Spirit within me, my heart cries out and calls You "Abba"—my dear and loving Father.

Accepted

*L*ord of heaven and earth, how I praise You that You are my perfect Father who fully accepts me as Your child through Christ, Your only begotten Son.

As someone who is in Christ and who belongs to You as Your very own, I thank You that I am fully accepted by You. For You "made us accepted in the Beloved." For Your Word tells me, "He has accepted you because of what the Lord Jesus Christ and the Spirit of our God have done for you."

Ephesians 1:6 NKJV; I Corinthians 6:11 TLB

I recognize that it isn't because I measure up on my own that You accept me—because I'm somehow innocent enough or strong enough or admirable enough. Rather, I rejoice in the truth that Jesus taught us—that You gladly associate with anyone who is willing to admit his sin and his spiritual need; You establish a permanent relationship with those who honestly seek Your deliverance, a relationship that excludes the possibility of being rejected. As Jesus said, "Those the Father has given me will come to me, and I will never reject them."

John 6:37 NLT

How amazing it is that You fully accept me even though You also fully know me—my weaknesses, sinfulness, and all. You are "intimately acquainted with all my ways." "He knows our frame; He remembers that we are dust." Yet You accept me now and forever.

Psalms 139:3; 103:14 NKJV

I rejoice that Your full acceptance and knowledge of me means that I can fully trust You: "For how well he understands us and knows what is best for us at all times." What a loving Father we have!

Ephesians 1:8 TLB

Thank You that, through Your Son, I have both Your continual acceptance and Your approval. My righteousness in Christ is a position of approval, and this approval brings peace. "Having been justified by faith, we have peace with God through our Lord Jesus Christ." By Christ's sacrifice I can enter Your presence at any time, day or night, assured that You welcome and gladly hear me. So I come before You now to thank and praise and worship You.

Romans 5:1 NKJV

Thank You that because of Your continual acceptance of me, I can come into Your presence and be heard at any time. I rejoice in Your promises concerning this: "When the righteous cry for help, the LORD hears and delivers them out of all their troubles." "If we ask anything according to his will he hears us." "He hears the prayer of the righteous."

Psalm 34:17 ESV; 1 John 5:14 ESV; Proverbs 15:29

Thank You for warmly inviting us to come into Your presence and to keep on coming. Your Word tells me, "Pour out your heart before Him; God is a refuge for us." "Come boldly to the throne of our gracious God. There we will receive his mercy, and we will find grace to help us when we need it most."

Psalm 62:8; Hebrews 4:16 NLT

I rejoice in the refuge I find in You, Father—a safe refuge where I receive mercy for my failures and grace to help in every time of need. You are better to me than all I could ever hope for or dream of. "How great is the love the Father has lavished on us, that we should be called children of God! And that is what we are!"

1 John 3:1 NIV

Intensely Personal

hank You that the wonderful and many-sided belongingness You provide means that I can actually think of myself as Your bride, as Scripture encourages us to do: "For your Maker is your husband, the LORD of hosts is his name."

Isaiah 54:5 ESV

My wonderful Lord, I thank You for Your intensely personal love that has actually invited me to take Your hand in marriage! I have accepted Your proposal. And I know that You are and always will be entirely faithful to Your promise to betroth me to Yourself forever "in righteousness and justice, in lovingkindness and mercy," and "in faithfulness."

Hosea 2:19-20 NKJV

Thank You for the joy that this kind of spiritual intimacy brings both to me and to you: "As a bridegroom rejoices over his bride, so will your God rejoice over you."

Isaiah 62:5 NIV

I rejoice that my belongingness in You also means I can accept with certainty that I'm Your friend. I especially want to thank You for this. For in our friendship You reveal so much to me and share so much with me —so many of Your plans and desires and promises and commitments...so much about Yourself and so much about me.

I praise You for Your love in making the facts of this friendship so clear to us in Your Word. "The friendship of the LORD is for those who fear him, and he makes known to them his covenant." Thank You for these words of promise spoken by Jesus: "You are My friends if you do what I command you.... I have called you friends, for all things that I have heard from My Father I have made known to you." And for these words: "I stand at the door and knock. If you hear my voice and open the door, I will come in, and we will share a meal together as friends."

Psalm 25:14 ESV; John 15:14-15; Revelation 3:20 NLT

Thank You that my belongingness also means I can think of myself with certainty as a citizen of God's heavenly kingdom. For Your Word tells us that because of Christ, "Our citizenship is in heaven." Thank You for this assurance: "You are citizens along with all of God's holy people. You are members of God's family." I rejoice in the comforting words spoken by Your Son, Jesus, concerning this: "It is your Father's good pleasure to give you the kingdom." Thank You for this gift! Because of it, I acknowledge that "this world is not our permanent home; we are looking forward to a home yet to come." And in obedience to Your Word, I gladly express my gratitude "for receiving a kingdom that cannot be shaken."

Philippians 3:20 NKJV; Ephesians 2:19 NLT; Luke 12:32 ESV; Hebrews 13:14 NLT; 12:28 ESV

Thank You for the fresh delight I can find day by day in the many-sided belongingness I enjoy with You.

Worthy

*I*n You, my gracious Lord, I find true worthiness. Thank You that whenever I'm tempted to feel guilty or condemned or useless, I can come to You and Your truth. And I find that in Your eyes I'm highly valued, because Christ has made me clean and forgiven and good and right in my innermost being—in my true self.

The worth You provide me in Christ is amazing—and all the more so as I face the fact of my natural sinfulness and weakness. I praise You for Your mercy, and I acknowledge that I never outgrow the need to pray, "God, be merciful to me a sinner!" I still fall short of Your ideals and standards, so with David I pray, "LORD, be merciful to me; heal my soul, for I have sinned against You." And I rejoice in the mercy that You so richly and consistently provide.

Luke 18:13 NKJV; Psalm 41:4 NKJV

Thank You for rescuing me when I was deeply entrenched in spiritual deadness and lack of power and for resurrecting me to true significance and growing Christlikeness. Thank You that in my spirit, I've been impregnated with the life and righteousness of Christ because I've been born anew. I now share His worthiness. Although in the lower part of my being the "motions of sin" still stir, in the higher part I am righteous forever. Sin is no longer my nature or my master, and it no longer has any right to condemn me. Why? Because through trusting Christ, I died out of the old life and was born into the new. So I now can say, "In Christ, I'm all right as a person forever!"

Thank You for assuring me that I belong to You, and I praise You for the truth that You never lightly value what You own. You call Your people Your "treasured possession." That's what we are to You. "The LORD's portion is his people"; we are "the apple of his eye." We are God's "gloriously rich portion."

Exodus 19:5 NIV; Deuteronomy 32:9-10 ESV; Ephesians 1:18 Williams

You say to each one of us, "You are mine," and "you are precious in my eyes." You treasure each of us as Your created one: "It is He who has made us, and not we ourselves; we are His people and the sheep of His pasture."

Isaiah 43:1,4 ESV; Psalm 100:3 NKJV

I'm so grateful for this assurance that You treasure me, that I'm precious in Your eyes because You created me—and even more because You redeemed me at the cost of Your Son's precious blood. Thank You for this truth: "God paid a ransom to save you.... And the ransom he paid was not mere gold or silver. It was the precious blood of Christ, the sinless, spotless Lamb of God." "He has purchased us to be his own people."

1 Peter 1:18-19 NLT; Ephesians 1:14 NLT

Loved

hank You, Lord, that You have given me Your perfect love as my dwelling place, as my home, where my heart can be at rest. In Your wondrous love, I find a hiding place—a haven I never want to leave!

Father, I rejoice in the mirror of Your love where I can see so accurately who I truly am! Thank You for inviting us in Your Word to fully behold this love: "See how very much our Father loves us."

1 John 3:1 NLT

I rejoice in the rich promises of Your love that You give us throughout Your Word. You say, "The one the LORD loves rests between his shoulders." You are my Beloved, and I rest my head on Your shoulder, thankful that You will never abandon me, that You will never let me go. You'll never let anything separate me from Your measureless love revealed in Christ Jesus, my Lord. You say, "When you pass through the waters, I will be with you." You promise me, "I will not forget you."

Deuteronomy 33:12 NIV; Isaiah 43:2 NKJV; 49:15 NKJV

You promise us, "My love will know no bounds." I praise You for Your limitless and eternal love that is beyond description. Yet I cannot help but voice my praise to You for surrounding me now and forever with Your boundless love.

Hosea 14:4 NLT

Thank You for assuring me that You will never withhold Your love from me. Instead, You will lavish it on me more and more in all the ages to come! How I praise and adore You! I rejoice that Your love is permanent: "Nothing can ever separate us from God's love. Neither death nor life, neither angels nor demons, neither our fears for today nor our worries about tomorrow—not even the powers of hell can separate us from God's love. No power in the sky above or in the earth below—indeed, nothing in all creation will ever be able to separate us from the love of God that is revealed in Christ Jesus our Lord." Thank You for Your promise: "With everlasting love I will have compassion on you."

Romans 8:38-39 NLT; Isaiah 54:8 NLT

Thank You for assuring us of Your love again and again. You tell us, "You are precious in my eyes...and I love you." "My steadfast love shall not depart from you." "I have loved you with an everlasting love; therefore I have continued my faithfulness to you."

Isaiah 43:4 ESV; 54:10 ESV; Jeremiah 31:3 ESV

Father, thank You for giving us assurance of Your love through the words of Your Son, Jesus: "The Father tenderly loves you." "As the Father loved Me, I also have loved you; abide in My love." Your love gives me lasting confidence, for I can "know and rely on the love God has for us."

John 16:27 Williams; 15:9 NKJV; I John 4:16 NIV

With loving confidence I gladly acknowledge Your nearness. "I will fear no evil; for You are with me." "In the shadow of Your wings I will make my refuge." "I am continually with You; You hold me by my right hand." You stay near to us to dine with us in the intimate fellowship enjoyed by dearest friends, for "our fellowship is with the Father and with His Son Jesus Christ." You are at home within me, and You surround me all day long.

Psalms 23:4 NKJV; 57:1 NKJV; 73:23 NKJV; I John 1:3 NKJV

I thank You especially for the incomparable proof of Your love for me in Christ. "God proves His love for us by the fact that Christ died for us."

Romans 5:8 Williams

Therefore to all those around me I can testify, "He has brought me to his banquet hall, and his banner over me is love."

Song of Solomon 2:4

Delighted in, Favored, and Honored

*D*ear Father, how glad I am that You not only love me—You also like me. You find delight and pleasure in me. "Because of what Christ has done we have become gifts to God that he delights in." "For the LORD takes pleasure in His people." "The LORD delights in you."

Ephesians 1:11 TLB; Psalm 149:4; Isaiah 62:4 NKJV

I praise You that You delight in me with great gladness and "rejoice over me with joyful songs." As I realize this truth, I hear You whisper, "You have captivated my heart."

Zephaniah 3:17 NLT personalized; Song of Solomon 4:9 ESV

Thank You for the endless flow of favor that springs out of Your delight in me. "For the LORD God is a sun and shield; the LORD bestows favor and honor. No good thing does he withhold from those who walk uprightly." You tell me, "I have known you by name, and you have also found favor in My sight."

Psalm 84:11 ESV; Exodus 33:12

Thank You especially for the grace—the unmerited favor—that You pour out on me in Christ. This grace makes me want to exclaim, "Look how the Eternal marks me out for favor!" "Surely, O LORD, you bless the righteous; you surround them with your favor as with a shield."

Psalms 4:3 Moffatt; 5:12 NIV

I rejoice in the never-ending flow of favor and honor that You send from Your heart to mine. Thank You for the rewards You promise for loving obedience on my part—for good deeds that are simply an extension of Your never-ending grace—and rewards that help display Your attribute of always being a Giver. Thank You that Your favor includes showing Your appreciation for specific things I do in serving You—even small things—and You promise to reward me for them. "God is not so unjust as to forget the work you have done and the love you have shown His name in the service you have rendered for your fellow-Christians, and still are doing." Thank You for this promise to me: "Nothing you do for the Lord is ever useless."

Hebrews 6:10 Williams; 1 Corinthians 15:58 NLT

Thank You that in all the labor I do for You, I can say with confidence, "I will trust God for my reward." For Your Word promises, "Whatever good anyone does, this he will receive back from the Lord." "Surely there is a reward for the righteous." And Jesus said, "Whoever gives one of these little ones only a cup of cold water in the name of a disciple, assuredly, I say to you, he shall by no means lose his reward."

Isaiah 49:4 NLT; Ephesians 6:8 ESV; Psalm 58:11 NKJV; Matthew 10:42 NKJV

Royalty

*L*ord God, I worship You as my King—as the King of kings—and I give You thanks for calling me out of this fallen world and bringing me into Your kingdom and Your family. You invite me into Your throne room as a royal child to spend time with You there. And You assure me of access to Your throne forever and ever.

What an honor it is that You make us royalty in Christ—sons and daughters of the King of kings. For Jesus Himself "has made us kings." We who are alive with Christ's righteousness can now live all our lives like kings! What a high privilege! What an exalted position!

Revelation 1:6 NKJV; Romans 5:17 Phillips

Thank You for this promise from Jesus Christ: "Those who are victorious will sit with me on my throne, just as I was victorious and sat with my Father on his throne."

Revelation 3:21 NLT

I confess that before I knew Christ, I was a spiritual pauper, needing to fight for my own rights and push my way through life. I was clothed in various kinds of rags—such as whining, coaxing, self-pity, anger, resentment, revenge. I tried to borrow from others the kind of love I desperately needed—discovering too often that they were paupers too! I went through garbage pails looking for scraps of self-realization. I tried to find an identity I could accept, a feeling that I was truly and unshakably somebody important. I tried to elbow my way to the top of the ash heap of visible status. I sought for a position above (or at least equal to) someone I was competing with. Or I just sat at the bottom of the heap, resenting those who were higher up.

But now I recognize how the attitudes that are expected from paupers or beggars are unbecoming to royalty—and unnecessary. I can now be liberated from them, because You, my King, hold me in highest favor. You promise to look out for my welfare and my true rights, to defend me, and to work things out for me.

How grateful I am that in Christ I never need to live as a pauper, not even for a moment. Thank You for delivering me from spiritual poverty and shame into Your very own royal richness and honor! Thank You for this truth about You: "He withdraws not His eyes from the righteous (the upright in right standing with God); but He sets them forever with kings upon the throne, and they are exalted."

Job 36:7 AMP

Nurtured, Satisfied, and Secure

O Lord my Shepherd, I worship You as the One who perfectly cares for me so that I never need to be anxious. Because You're so rich—with unlimited resources—I can live free from anxiety, knowing that my every need will be fully met. And when anxiety overtakes me, I have in Christ the solution.

Thank You for making this so clear in Your Word: "Seek the Kingdom of God above all else, and live righteously, and he will give you everything you need." "God will supply every need of yours according to his riches in glory in Christ Jesus." Thank You for affirming that You care for me, and that therefore "I can throw the whole weight of my anxieties upon him, for I am his personal concern."

Matthew 6:33 NLT; Philippians 4:19 ESV; 1 Peter 5:7 Phillips personalized

How I praise You for Your inexhaustible care and concern, and I thank You for the security and stability they give me. "We are the people he watches over, the flock under his care." "He will feed His flock like a shepherd." And You feed us "with the finest of wheat; and with honey from the rock."

Psalm 95:7 NLT; Isaiah 40:11 NKJV; Psalm 81:16 NKJV

I praise You for being so constant and thorough and deliberate in Your care for me and all Your children. After describing Your people as Your vineyard, You say, "I, the LORD, am its keeper; every moment I water it…. I keep it night and day." You tell us, "I, the LORD, made you, and I will not forget you"; "I made you, and I will care for you." And You keep inviting us to "taste and see" that You are good.

Isaiah 27:3 ESV; 44:21 NLT; 46:4 NLT; Psalm 34:8

Thank You that every day I can experience Your care and nurture in unique ways, for Your "tender compassions…are new every morning." You satisfy me "with good so that my youth is renewed like the eagle's."

Lamentations 3:22-23 AMP; Psalm 103:5 ESV personalized

Your Word promises me that Jesus, as the church's Bridegroom, "nourishes and cherishes" us. Therefore I can say with contentment, "The LORD is my shepherd, I shall not be in want."

Ephesians 5:29 NKJV; Psalm 23:1 NIV

You promise that Your people will be satisfied with Your goodness. So I affirm to You that I am "abundantly satisfied with the fullness of Your house" as I gladly "drink from the river of Your pleasures." "You satisfy me more than the richest feast. I will praise you with songs of joy."

Jeremiah 31:14; Psalms 36:8 NKJV; 63:5 NLT

Lord, I also praise and worship You for being my Strength, my Champion, my Defender. I rejoice in Your assurance: "Yes, I will help you, I will uphold you with My righteous right hand." Thank You for the limitless power and wisdom that You bring to bear on my problems and difficulties. You truly are "an ever-present help in trouble." In Your sovereign care I'm guarded from every threat and unmet need. For You are the

God of all grace, You have called me to Your eternal glory in Christ, and You have promised to "restore, confirm, strengthen, and establish" me.

Isaiah 41:10 NKJV; Psalm 46:1 NIV; 1 Peter 5:10 ESV

Your promise is sure: "The Lord is faithful, and he will strengthen and protect you from the evil one." You are able to keep me from stumbling and to make me stand in the presence of Your glory "blameless with great joy."

2 Thessalonians 3:3 NIV; Jude 24

Therefore I can say with confidence, "My help comes from the LORD." "Blessed be the Lord, who daily bears me up." "In peace I will both lie down and sleep, for You alone, O LORD, make me to dwell in safety." With David, I can testify of You, "He only is my rock and my salvation, my stronghold; I shall not be greatly shaken." You "set my feet upon a rock, making my steps secure."

Psalms 121:2 NKJV; 68:19 ESV personalized; 4:8; 62:2; 40:2 ESV

Therefore, Lord, I can affirm with Paul, "I know whom I have trusted and I am absolutely sure that He is able to guard what I have entrusted to Him." Just as Paul did, I choose to trust You to guard and rescue me from every danger and to bring me safely home into Your eternal kingdom.

2 Timothy 1:12 Williams; 4:18 ESV

Competent

I praise You, Lord God, that through my new birth in Christ, You have begun to make me competent and adequate for the future You have planned for me. In all that You are, I can find complete sufficiency for all that awaits me. I can say with Paul and with every believer, "Our sufficiency is from God."

2 Corinthians 3:5 NKJV

Thank You for Your promise to transform me. For as Your children behold You, "All of us...are being transformed into likeness to Him, from one degree of splendor to another, since it comes from the Lord who is the Spirit." Thank You that this change in me—this Christian growth and transformation—rests from beginning to end on Your loving work within me, as Your Word explains: "He Himself works in you and accomplishes that which is pleasing in His sight, through Jesus Christ."

2 Corinthians 3:18 Williams; Hebrews 13:21 AMP

Thank You that no matter what faults and personal struggles I now face, I can cultivate this thought pattern: "I can change! I can become more than I am. I can develop a greater ability to cope with life and especially to relate to other people in a more positive and significant way." I rejoice in the truth that righteous, holy living is consistent with the person I now am. It isn't something foreign to me that I have to produce out of duty or even gratefulness. Rather, as I choose to follow Christ, I can expect to live a holy life because of who Christ is, what He has done, and what He has made me through my new birth. My competence is the outflow of Christ's life in me.

What a thrill it is to know that the relational truths that belonged to God's people in the Old Testament now apply to me. I am uniquely beautiful in Your sight, for You see me through eyes of love as a bridegroom sees his bride, focusing on the positives. And as I grow spiritually and delight in Your perfections, Your promise is that the beauty I have from You will continue to deepen and intensify: "You will also be a crown of beauty in the hand of the LORD, and a royal diadem in the hand of your God."

Isaiah 62:3

Yes, the best is yet to come! I look forward with confidence to what You will accomplish in me and through me. "For because of our faith, he has brought us into this place of highest privilege where we now stand, and we confidently and joyfully look forward to actually becoming all that God has had in mind for us to be." "For we are God's masterpiece. He has created us anew in Christ Jesus, so we can do the good things he planned for us long ago."

Romans 5:2 TLB; Ephesians 2:10 NLT

Thank You especially for loving me enough to discipline and train me, for as You continually teach and refine me, I'll more and more fulfill my God-designed destiny as Your masterpiece. Thank You for the truth that "the Lord disciplines the one he loves." Along the way, You don't expect from me perfect performance or an ideal personality, nor do You condemn me for my failures. "For He knows our frame; He remembers that we are dust."

Hebrews 12:6 ESV; Psalm 103:14 NKJV

How good to know that what You expect from me is realistic. So I thank You for the high, challenging goals and standards You call me to in holiness and righteousness, and You continually help me grow in measuring up to them. With Paul I can say, "Not that I have already obtained this or am already perfect, but I press on to make it my own, because Christ Jesus has made me his own.... I press on toward the goal for the prize of the upward call of God in Christ Jesus."

Philippians 3:12,14 ESV

Bold and Confident

*L*ord God, You are my Liberator and Savior. Thank You for setting me free from the disabling power of sin and death and for giving me a life of fresh, new boldness in You. Thank You for the opportunity You give me to rise up and soar ever higher in this new liberty. I know that the more I give You the controls of my life, the freer I will be.

Thank You for letting me experience a basic breakthrough into freedom—from "ought to" living into the joy of simply living out Christ's life, letting Him display His life in and through me. For He grants me freedom from sin's crippling restraints. Thank You for Your word of freedom to me: "You live under the freedom of God's grace.... You are free from your slavery to sin."

Romans 6:14,18 NLT

I rejoice that my freedom is Spirit produced and Spirit sustained: "For the Lord is the Spirit, and wherever the Spirit of the Lord is, there is freedom." I glory in this truth: "The life-giving principles of the Spirit have freed you in Christ Jesus from the control of the principles of sin and death."

2 Corinthians 3:17 NLT; Romans 8:2 MLB

Therefore with boldness I can say to You, "O LORD, truly I am your servant...you have freed me from my chains.... I run in the path of your commands, for you have set my heart free.... I will walk about in freedom, for I have sought out your precepts."

Psalms 116:16 NIV; 119:32,45 NIV

As I consider how limited and vulnerable I am, how encouraging it is to hear You say, "My grace is sufficient for you, for My strength is made perfect in weakness"! As Your power rests upon me and governs me, I can say with assurance, "When I am weak, then I am strong." What a privilege it is to "say with confidence, 'The LORD is my helper, so I will have no fear.'" I rejoice in the truth of Your strength for me: "It is God who arms me with strength, and makes my way perfect." And I affirm, "I am ready for anything through the strength of the One who lives within me."

2 Corinthians 12:9-10 NKJV; Hebrews 13:6 NLT; Psalm 18:32 NKJV; Philippians 4:13 Phillips

Therefore I praise You by telling You personally, "You…made me bold with strength in my soul." "My heart is confident, O God; my heart is confident." I rejoice in Your promise: "The LORD will be your confidence." And in this one: "Your confidence…has great reward."

Psalms 138:3 NKJV; 57:7 MLB; Proverbs 3:26 ESV; Hebrews 10:35 NKJV

Thank You that I'm on the winning side; I'm an eternal victor with You. In Christ, strength and triumph are mine, and I no longer have to yield to defeatism. "God…always leads us in triumph in Christ." I can face the future with boldness and without fear, knowing that You will give the strength I need to be an overcomer in any trial, for in Christ I am guaranteed victory: "Overwhelming victory is ours through Christ, who loved us." I am an overcomer "because He who is in me is greater than he who is in the world." I've been born of God, and "whatever is born of God overcomes the world."

2 Corinthians 2:14 NKJV; Romans 8:37 NLT; I John 4:4 NKJV personalized; 5:4 NKJV

Thank You especially for Your wise and trustworthy guidance as day by day You lead me in "paths of righteousness for [Your] name's sake." I can be confident in Your guidance and instruction as You lead me into a life of true wisdom. "For the LORD gives wisdom." "He leads the humble in what is right, and teaches the humble his way." "He will show them the path they should choose." With David I can say, "You teach me wisdom in the inmost place."

Psalm 23:3; Proverbs 2:6; Psalms 25:9 ESV; 25:12 NLT; 51:6 NIV

Thank You for granting this guidance in personal ways as I hear You say to me, "I am the LORD your God, who teaches you what is best for you, who directs you in the way you should go." And this: "I will guide you along the best pathway for your life. I will advise you and watch over you." Thank You for this promise: "Your ears shall hear a word behind you, saying, 'This is the way, walk in it,' whenever you turn to the right hand or whenever you turn to the left."

Isaiah 48:17 NIV; Psalm 32:8 NLT; Isaiah 30:21 NKJV

Thank You for the inner simplicity of following You that will grow within me as I learn to depend more constantly on the indwelling life of Christ, counting on Him for wisdom and strength.

Purposeful

I worship and praise You, Lord God, for including me in Your glorious eternal purposes. Thank You for the thrilling sense of significance this gives to me—the assurance that in Your service I can live a life of love and adventure and fruitfulness. Thank You for the part I can share in communicating to others Your exciting plans and purposes.

Thank You especially for the incredible freedom You give me to truly love others and the exalted privilege of being a channel of Your supernatural love flowing freely to those around me. I acknowledge You as my Teacher of love, for as Your children we "have been [personally] taught by God to love one another." Thank You that the very freedom I have in the Spirit is a freedom to love—for we "have been called to live in freedom…freedom to serve one another in love."

I Thessalonians 4:9 AMP; Galatians 5:13 NLT

Thank You for the vast possibilities for growing in love, for Your Word shows us this potential—"to increase and excel and overflow in love for one another and for all people"; You help us envision a love that "may overflow still more and more, directed by fuller knowledge and keener insight."

I Thessalonians 3:12 AMP; Philippians 1:9 Williams

I exult in knowing that You allow me to be Your ambassador, with Your love as the driving force behind my calling to be a witness for Christ to both believers and unbelievers. "The love of Christ controls and urges and impels us, because we are of the opinion and conviction that...One died for all...so that all those who live might live no longer to and for themselves, but to and for Him Who died and was raised again for their sake."

2 Corinthians 5:14-15 AMP

From Christ's presence within me, You want to manifest through me the fragrance that results from knowing You. Why do I qualify for this exciting privilege? Only because I am in Christ and He is in me. As Paul wrote, "It pleased God...to reveal His Son in me." "[It is He] Who has qualified us [making us to be fit and worthy and sufficient] as ministers and dispensers of a new covenant [of salvation through Christ]."

2 Corinthians 2:14 MLB; Galatians 1:15-16 NKJV; 2 Corinthians 3:6 AMP

I acknowledge that with my assortment of inadequacies, I fulfill my high calling as a witness for Christ not by trying to be what I'm not but by realizing who I am in Christ, then depending on You to let my true inner self shine forth. From a human viewpoint, I'm not qualified, for I lack many longed-for qualities, abilities, and talents. Yet from Your viewpoint, I am qualified: "For the LORD does not see as man sees; for man looks at the outward appearance, but the LORD looks at the heart." And as You keep refining and humbling me, Your life and message will come through more and more clearly in my actions and words, and others will sense Your fragrant aroma in me.

1 Samuel 16:7 NKJV; 2 Corinthians 2:14

Embracing a Glorious Future

*M*y loving God, how I praise and adore You for being constantly at work to fulfill Your gracious purposes in me. Every day is alive with Your fresh acts of mercy as You move me forward in fulfilling Your plans for my life. Your working means I am becoming like a mighty oak, "the planting of the LORD, that he may be glorified." I can say with confidence, "The LORD will fulfill His purpose for me." I can count on Your promise: "There is surely a future hope for you, and your hope will not be cut off."

Isaiah 61:3 ESV; Psalm 138:8 ESV; Proverbs 23:18 NIV

Thank You for Your good purposes that undergird all that happens to me. I'm especially grateful to know that You are leading me on the path to perfect holiness, to full freedom from the presence of sin in the eternal glory You have called me to. In my innermost being, Christ's sacrifice has already made me "forever perfect." In Him, my holiness is something I've already received: "We have been made holy (consecrated and sanctified) through the offering made once for all of the body of Jesus Christ (the Anointed One)." I am so grateful that I can continue to experience this holiness as You keep working in my daily life, conforming my mind, my emotions, and my will to the image of Christ. You Yourself will "put the finishing touches on me."

Hebrews 10:14 TLB; 10:10 AMP; 2 Corinthians 5:5 Williams

I praise You for the blend of trials and blessings that You are using to prepare me to reign with You forever. I can be fully confident in how You shape my circumstances, both present and future, for You assure us that "to those who love God, who are called according to his plan, everything that happens fits into a pattern for good."

Romans 8:28 Phillips

How I rejoice in Your plans to bring me to glory. I will see You face to face, for You have promised me the supreme privilege: "Your eyes will see the King in His beauty." And You will share with me Your matchless glory: "We know that when He appears, we will be like Him, because we will see Him just as He is."

Isaiah 33:17 NKJV; 1 John 3:2

My hope will be perfectly fulfilled on that day when You are revealed to us in all Your glory. I will finally be all that Christ Jesus saved me for and longs for me to be. That day "will mean splendour unimaginable. It will be a breath-taking wonder to all who believe." "An eternal weight of glory" will be mine. Thank You for this unimaginable and unending splendor that I will enjoy.

Philippians 3:12 NLT; 2 Thessalonians 1:10 Phillips; 2 Corinthians 4:17 ESV

A Life of Praise and Victory

Commander of Victories

*F*ather in heaven, I lift up my heart to You as the gracious and almighty Ruler of all things everywhere. How grateful I am that You have given us the powerful weapons of prayer and praise to help win victories over our spiritual enemies.

Thank You that prayer and praise give me constant opportunities to be on active duty in the spiritual war that surrounds us. How glad I am, my King and my God, that through prayer I can influence You to command victories near and far—in my own life and service, in the lives of those around me, and in those laboring for You in the far corners of the earth. Through prayer and praise I can help them be strong in faith and bold in their witness even when Satan seeks to sift them as wheat. What a privilege this is!

Psalm 44:4; Luke 22:31-32

I worship You as our supreme Ruler, sovereign over all. You are all-powerful and all-wise. You are exalted far above all powers and rulers, both good and evil, visible and invisible. I praise You that You reign over all, with never the slightest alarm about the powers of evil, for Your throne is never threatened.

1 Chronicles 29:11-12

Thank You that You are infinitely greater than that old serpent, the devil, who started this millenniums-long war against You, trying to usurp

Your authority and power. I rejoice that ages ago You cast him out of Your headquarters in heaven. And You are constantly working all things according to the counsel of Your will, including everything regarding our Enemy. You never look back and say, "Oops, I shouldn't have allowed Satan to do that." Century after century he operates only under You and in ultimate subjection to Your purposes.

Revelation 12:9; Ephesians 1:11

So I take my stand in You as the One who is sovereign over all evil influences. I count on You as a shield around me. I stand against the works of the flesh and the enticements of the world that so easily distract me and hinder my prayers. I choose to put off the filthy clothes of fleshly living—the selfishness, the lust, the distrust, the neglect of my privilege of prayer. As Your chosen child, I put on the beautiful garments You've provided through the life of Christ in me. I give You thanks for my weakness, and I glory in the truth that Your strength is made perfect in weakness—that out of my weakness You are making me strong.

1 John 2:15-17; Colossians 3:10 NLT; 2 Corinthians 12:9

Victory Design

*H*ow I praise You, Ruler of the ages, that You've brought me into the stream of Your purposes—into Your glorious plan. You've taught me to yield all my allegiance to You as my King. And You've enlisted me into Your army to join Your people in doing battle under Your sovereign rule. You're counting on all Your children to be involved in this ages-long battle to defeat Satan, turning people from his kingdom to Yours—"to open their eyes so that they may turn from darkness to light and from the dominion of Satan to God." So I rejoice and pray, focusing on Your unparalleled power and Your glorious eternal plans.

2 Timothy 2:3; 1 Timothy 4:12; Acts 26:18

You are the living Rock, solid and unshakable. Your glorious power surrounds me, overshadows me, and prepares the way before me. You are my Strength and Shield, my Saving Defense and Refuge, my Sure Footing, and my all-sufficient God who is enough. You make me steadfast and immovable! I worship You as the greatest, most awesome of all beings—more impressive, more powerful than anything on earth. You are exalted high above any hindrances or adversaries that loom large in my life right now, whether in my personality or my present circumstances or my future.

Deuteronomy 32:4; Psalm 28:7; 1 Corinthians 15:58

You, Lord God, are Yahweh Most High, the great King over all the earth. You are the Overcomer, the almighty Conqueror, able to win overwhelming victories. And You are my sanctuary, the holy, secluded, safe place where I can enter and be at rest in Your strength. Thank You that I can conquer because I trust in You!

Psalms 97:9; 47:2-3; 62:7; 2 Chronicles 13:18

I exult that You are seated in the heavenlies, high above all Enemy powers, and I am seated with You! So in my battles with Satan I can come at him from above. I shout to You with a voice of joy and triumph, for You're the One who subdues the Enemy under my feet.

Ephesians 1:20-22; 2:6; Psalm 47:1,3

For everything I need, what a privilege it is to go right to the top— to the supreme Authority, the highest Ruler, who is all-powerful and all-loving—to the One who deeply cares about my well-being and loves me with a perfect love. To the best of my knowledge, I surrender wholly to You. And I trust You to continue Your gracious work of cleansing and transforming my life—of sanctifying me wholly, spirit, soul, and body.

Romans 12:1; 1 Thessalonians 5:23

Greater

*F*ather, I lift my heart in worship, for You are the great and awesome God. I ascribe to You glory and strength; I give to You the glory that You deserve; I worship You in the beauty of holiness.

Psalm 29:1-2

I stand in awe of You, for Your voice is powerful. You are the One who speaks and it is done, as You demonstrated when You created the universe. Thank You for Your voice of authority that terrifies our enemies as we rely on You and for the blows of Your arm that they cannot escape.

Psalms 33:8-10; 2:5; 98:1

How great and mighty You are, infinitely more powerful than any human might. You are immeasurably stronger than all military forces and all weapons, even the most devastating. Your might is unlimited, unbounded, far beyond anything we can imagine. You are well able to destroy all the schemes and plots and works of Satan. And Your power is a loving power, able to turn into blessing even the worst that Satan does.

2 Chronicles 20:6; Psalm 62:11-12

How unnerving it is, Lord, to see the crafty ways Satan tries to weaken our faith and destroy our walk with You. But I worship You as the strongest Strong One. You are the Lord of hosts—of vast spiritual armies, infinitely greater than Satan and his legions of evil spirits. Thank

You that praising and worshiping You stimulates my faith and makes my spiritual enemies cringe in defeat.

Job 9:19; Isaiah 2:12; Psalm 8:2

You are the living God, the God of mighty victories, the God of both heaven and earth. You are enthroned higher than the highest angels. And You alone are God of all the kingdoms of the earth. I count on You to work in this world in ways that will hasten Your purposes and cause countless people to trust Christ as their Savior and Lord.

Jeremiah 10:10; Psalm 57:5

Thank You for Christ's promise that those who believe in Him would do even greater works than He did in His ministry on earth. In this continuing war against Satan, enable me to fulfill the purposes You have for me, both small and great—through prayer, through using my spiritual gifts, and through being a witness for You to unbelievers as well as to people who already know You.

John 14:12

I pray especially about the following needs and opportunities, both near and far:

To You, Father, "the only God our Savior, through Jesus Christ our Lord, be glory, majesty, dominion and authority…now and forever. Amen."

Jude 25

The Power of Your Goodness

*H*ow glad I am, Lord, that the basic secret for overcoming our Enemy is simply knowing You in a vital and deepening relationship. Thank You that the more I let You meet my needs, the less vulnerable I am to temptation and the stronger I am to do Your will.

Acts 20:29-32; 2 Peter 1:3-4; 3:18

I praise You that You are exalted high above all. You're the Ruler over everything and everyone. This would be a terrifying thought if You were evil or if You had evil streaks in Your nature. But how assuring it is to know that You are altogether holy and righteous and loving—a wise God who knows all things and always wills the best for us. I honor You for being totally good in Your character, and I'm so glad that Your will for us is also totally good. You always have the best purposes in mind for whatever You bring into our lives or allow to happen. What stability we have in You!

Psalm 89:11-14; Deuteronomy 32:4; Jeremiah 29:11

And how grateful I am that You are eternal. You look beyond today as You allow things in our lives that help us become our best, both for our future here on earth and for eternity. I praise You that even Satan's attacks and his efforts to sidetrack us come by Your permission to help accomplish in and for us the very things he hates.

Psalm 90:2; 1 Timothy 1:17; Psalm 66:10

Thank You that the good name of Your Son, Jesus, is far above all other names—that behind it is the boundless power of His Cross and Resurrection and Ascension. I rejoice that Satan trembles before this matchless name. The war has been won, and we're simply bringing in the spoils!

Ephesians 1:19-21

So I praise You for the great privilege of knowing You and walking with You and experiencing Your presence with me and in me. Place in my heart a deeper desire to know You better, to live in constant fellowship with You, and to walk worthy of my calling. When I get diverted or distracted or indifferent, cause me to quickly return to a simple trust and delight in You. Make me quickly aware when a spiritual enemy—whether Satan's forces or my flesh or the world—draws me away from You and Your sufficiency. I count on You to bind Satan when he seeks to hinder Your gracious purposes for my life.

Ephesians 4:1; Colossians 1:9-10

I pray You'll do these same things in the lives of Your servants, especially:

Exalted Lamb, Defeated Foe

ow I rejoice, Father, that You have seated the Man, Christ Jesus, in the position of highest power at Your right hand. How grateful I am for the agony that You and He went through to make this possible. You let Your beloved Son leave heaven's glory to be born in a stable, cradled in a feeding trough, entrusted to a poor couple from a despised city. Then You let Him suffer on the cross, despised and rejected, bearing all the sin and sorrows of all the ages. How I rejoice that by dying, He broke the power of the devil, including the power of death, so that He could liberate us from slavery to sin and from the fear of dying. Then You sealed Your Son's triumph by raising Him from the dead (death could not keep its prey!) and lifting Him to His exalted place far above all other powers, putting all things in subjection under His feet.

Isaiah 53:2-6; Hebrews 2:14-15; Ephesians 1:20-22

So I worship Your Son, the Lamb who shed His blood for all my sin, the Lamb exalted at Your right hand. How worthy He is of my praise! "Your right hand, O LORD, has become glorious in power; Your right hand, O LORD, has dashed the enemy in pieces."

Revelation 5:12; Exodus 15:6 NKJV

I praise You that the day will come when Jesus will abolish all rule and authority and power, and with our eyes we'll actually see all enemies put under His feet. Then He'll deliver the kingdom up to You, Father, that You may be all in all.

1 Corinthians 15:24-28

I rejoice that because our Lord Jesus disarmed the devil and canceled his authority, our Enemy is now a wounded beast headed for eternal punishment. He is a defeated foe, along with his army of demons! How glad I am that You've pronounced the judicial verdict against them, though their final defeat has not yet been carried out. In Your great wisdom and long-range purposes, You allow the Enemy a degree of freedom to deceive and attack human beings on the earth—but only until his final and eternal punishment in the lake of fire. Even now it's only under Your sovereign power and wisdom that he's able to prowl the earth.

Colossians 2:15; Revelation 20:2,10

I'm so grateful that You, my all-powerful God, are in supreme control and that You protect me as I put my faith in Your Son's triumph over all the forces of evil. Thank You that I can count on You to give continuing and overwhelming victory through our Lord Jesus Christ.

Romans 8:37; 1 Corinthians 15:57

That Day!

*F*ather, I rejoice at the day when all evil and all evil powers will be destroyed. "Let the heavens be glad, and let the earth rejoice; let the sea roar, and all it contains; let the field exult, and all that is in it. Then all the trees of the forest will sing for joy before the LORD, for He is coming, for He is coming to judge the earth."

Psalm 96:11-13

At the time of Satan's rebellion, You could have spoken the word and utterly destroyed both him and his fallen angels. Or You could have banished him forever after the fall of Adam and Eve. Instead You've allowed him broad influence and control. Who, Lord, can fully understand Your wisdom, which is so complex, so many-sided?

Romans 11:33

I come to sit at Your feet, to listen with my heart as I read Your Word. I come to pour out my love, to worship and bow down. I kneel before You, my Maker, for You are my God, and I am a sheep of Your pasture. How grateful I am that I'm Yours! Splendor and majesty, strength and beauty are in Your sanctuary, and I have the privilege of dwelling there! My innermost being is Your holy place—a place of majestic holiness and moral beauty, a place that's eternally undefiled.

Psalms 95:6-7; 100:3; 96:6

I praise You that though at times You may grant the devil power over my circumstances and even over my body, he has no power over my present and eternal relationship with You. And how wonderful to be on Your side—on the winning side! I rejoice that the day will come when every knee shall bow to Christ and every tongue will confess that He is Lord, to Your glory as God the Father. I worship You because Your grace has been revealed, bringing salvation to all people, and so we can look forward to that wonderful event when the glory of our great God and Savior, Jesus Christ, will be revealed.

Philippians 2:10-11; Titus 2:11-13

I honor Your name; I pray that Your will may be done this day in my life and in my sphere of influence. Fill my heart with the confident hope of Your coming kingdom, and keep me focused on advancing that glorious kingdom today.

Matthew 6:10

I pray that Satan will be defeated in all he wants to do in the following situations:

Safe from Accusation

I praise You, my glorious and exalted God, that when Your Son rose from the grave and ascended into heaven, You raised *me* with Him! I'm now seated with Christ in the heavenly realms! He shares with me His position at Your right hand—a position of supreme power and victory and unbelievably close fellowship with You.

Ephesians 2:6

This is my privilege, Father, as a citizen of heaven—part of the birthright that became mine on that wonderful day I became a member of Your family. All this was part of Your eternal plan for all who trust Your Son as their Savior and Master. You determined these blessings for us even before You founded the earth. Thank You that I can be confident of my exalted position and enjoy it increasingly as I count on these truths.

Philippians 3:20; Ephesians 1:3-5

So now I'm Your servant, Lord, committed to live for Your glory. I ask You to live out Your life in me with Your love and limitless power. Give me the grace and strength to more and more constantly let You be the answer to my every need…my every shortcoming…my every opportunity to glorify You. Work in me both to will and to do what pleases You.

Psalms 116:16; 86:16; Philippians 2:13

I want to give You abundant thanksgiving and praise that I'm Your chosen one, and therefore the Enemy cannot succeed in accusing me before You. He may try to bring a charge against me for my sins, but he will fail, for they've all been forgiven—past, present, and future. "Who is in a position to condemn? Only Christ Jesus, and Christ died for me, Christ also rose for me, Christ reigns in power for me, Christ prays for me!"

Romans 8:33-34 Phillips personalized

Now, Lord, though Satan loves to condemn me and bring charges against me, I need never grovel in the dust with chains around my neck. How I praise You for this! You have broken those chains! You have cleansed me and given me new garments of righteousness and praise instead of despair. So day by day I can rise up, put on those beautiful garments, and worship You in holy array—in the beauty of holiness.

Isaiah 61:3,10; 52:1-2; Psalm 29:2

How grateful I am, Father, for how these truths are mine to believe and meditate on. I thank You for the way they help me maintain my victory over Satan and his evil powers. May this victory become more full and constant in my life—and in my fellow believers, especially:

Shake Off the Dust

*V*ictory—what a word, Lord! A word full of meaning: overwhelming triumph, eternal and complete. And how grateful I am that Christ's victory is mine—part of the position and privileges that You gave me when I became Yours.

I praise You that no demons—no ruling spirits of any kind—now have any authority over me. How amazing and glorious that all my spiritual enemies have been judged and exposed as losers, eternally defeated losers. I no longer need to fear them, though I still need to resist them as I draw near to You day by day, hour by hour.

Romans 8:37-39; Colossians 2:15

Because You've prepared me in Christ for victories over the Enemy, I shake off the dust and rise up. I loose myself from any bondage of the flesh or of Satan, and I put on the Lord Jesus Christ, clothing myself with Him as my strength.

Isaiah 52:1-2; Romans 13:14

Thank You, Lord, that Your name—Your wonderful, all-powerful name!—is a strong tower where I can be safe and encouraged. You are my Rock, my Refuge, and my Rescuer. You give me a way to escape from the attacks of all my spiritual enemies, from the unseen spiritual rulers and authorities of this world's darkness. Thank You for giving me in Christ a place of safety and protection. As one of Your loved ones, I can rest in Your arms; I can lie down in safety, close to You, assured that You protect me all night long as well as all day long. What promises and privileges are mine!

Proverbs 18:10; Psalm 71:3; Deuteronomy 33:12 NCV

You are my strength every morning, my salvation in times of distress. You're the stability of my times. So I clothe myself with my beautiful garment of praise. I treasure the safety You've provided from any crafty attacks by the Enemy—from anything that would not be for my ultimate good or for the advance of the good news. Even when You allow severe trials in my life, You know my path, and when You have tried me, I shall come forth as gold.

Isaiah 33:2; 61:3; Romans 8:28; Philippians 1:12; Job 23:10

I pray that in new ways and with greater constancy my life will be victorious. May I be a glory to Your name hour by hour, defeating Satan's purposes regardless of what happens. And I pray the same for all Your children and servants—especially:

Victory as We Testify

I glorify You, Father, for You are exalted on high, far above all evil powers, and You've given me victory over the devil who accuses Your people day and night. What a privilege that I can pray with confidence and stand firmly against the ways the Enemy tries to accuse or condemn or discredit me.

Revelation 12:10

You are my Strength and Glory; through You I can repel the onslaught of the Enemy. I praise You that the keys to victory are mine as I let You be the Lord of my life—as by simple faith I depend on the death and resurrected life of Your Son. How I thank You that His tremendous power is available to me!

Isaiah 28:5-6; Ephesians 1:19 Phillips

Thank You too for the critical blow that came to Satan when Jesus shed His blood for my sins, dying in my place to pay the penalty I deserved—then rising from the dead, ascending to glory, and coming to live in and through each believer. You clothe me with strength so I can resist my enemies—the world with its lust and pride, the flesh, and the devil with his temptations and accusations.

John 12:31; 16:11; 1 John 2:16

I praise You for how Your Spirit fills us with power and courage to speak the truth of the gospel. Thank You that He convicts people of sin, convinces them of truth through the crucified and risen Christ, and releases them from the power of Satan to God. How I rejoice that the evil ruler of this world has been judged!

Acts 26:18; John 16:8-11

I'm so grateful for the victories that come as we testify to believers as well as unbelievers, proclaiming the good news of our Savior's death and resurrection and kingly control. How I rejoice that our testimony and sharing of Your Word defeats Satan in the lives of people, both those he has blinded spiritually and believers he's seeking to ensnare.

Acts 1:8; 2 Corinthians 4:4

I gladly welcome these powerful, invisible weapons You've made available for us. I praise You that they have divine power to demolish strongholds and to take captive every thought, making it obedient to Christ—and that this includes my thoughts! Enable me to use these weapons wisely and continuously.

2 Corinthians 10:4-5

And I give You thanks, as the mighty Deliverer, for the way praise works to expel the power of the Evil One. Give me the grace to continue in praise and prayer until Satan is defeated in the following lives and situations:

My Part in the Battle
for Others

*T*hank You, Lord, for the part I can have in Your spiritual battle to rescue people from Satan's dark kingdom and to prepare them to reign with You forever. I praise You, Lord, for the challenging plan You have for my life. Thank You that this plan includes walking close to You, helping others know and enjoy this same closeness, and using my spiritual gift.

Acts 26:18; Colossians 3:16-17; 1 Corinthians 7:7

I rejoice that You are mightily at work against the Enemy's purposes as he cleverly seeks to blind and destroy both believers and unbelievers. Empower me to do my part in this work and to endure opposition and hardship as Your soldier. Help me constantly rejoice that I'm on the winning side.

2 Timothy 2:3,10

You have shown us that the prince of the power of the air is actively at work in those who don't know and obey You—to blind them, to entice them to evil, and to use them against Your purposes and against Your servants. But You've promised that in You—in the power of Your might—we are strong, and we can call on You to release Your mighty power. You are our refuge and strength, a very present help in trouble—abundantly available to help in tight places. Thank You that this is true not only for us but for all who will come to faith in You and grow spiritually because of our testimony.

Ephesians 2:2; 6:10; Colossians 1:11; Psalm 46:1

Make me sensitive to people's needs. Grant me timely words for those who are weary and special grace to share with them the reason for the wonderful hope I have.

Isaiah 50:4; 1 Peter 3:15

With all the tensions and complaints and disputes in this world, even among Your people, thank You for asking me to be a peacemaker. Use me, Lord, to help heal broken hearts and broken relationships that divide families and churches and communities. All this division is not from You, Lord; it's from the devil himself, who loves to see Christians arguing and fighting and disunited. I worship You as the only one who can help Your people change this.

Philippians 2:14; James 3:18

I call on You, Lord, to work deeply in those who need greater unity—groups that I'm in touch with, such as:

Also people and families I'm concerned about, such as:

Do something special through Your Word and Your Spirit to heal wounds and unite hearts. How I praise You that Jesus is the Victor over Satan and his divisiveness.

Your Family

*T*hank You that You are the great, faithful God who longs to give each of Your children personal daily victories over the Evil One, as well as long-term victories. "O my soul, march on with strength."

Judges 5:21

Thank You for the inner strength that comes from knowing I can call You "Abba (Daddy), Father." And how amazing it is that Your Son is not ashamed to call us brothers and sisters. I rejoice that You—the awesome Creator of the universe and all things in it, including all people—have given us the privilege of actually being Your children, born of You, and included as members of Your royal family for all eternity!

Galatians 4:6; Hebrews 2:11; 1 John 3:1

I praise You that these privileges give me increasing strength and victory through our Lord Jesus Christ—victory over Satan and all his schemes, victory over the world system and all its corruption, and victory over my own fleshly nature and failings. What a privilege, what a joy divine to be able to lean with full confidence on Your everlasting arms, which enable me to thrust out the Enemy.

1 Corinthians 15:57; Deuteronomy 33:27

You are well able, Lord, to defeat my spiritual enemies, even as You defeated Israel's enemies in Old Testament times. In the name of Jesus, I count on You to demoralize these enemies. Confuse them, confound their strategies, and cause them to panic. Bring their plans to nothing.

Isaiah 19:2-3

Let all Your enemies perish, O Lord, but let everyone who loves You "be like the rising of the sun in its might." Thank You that Christ has delivered me from the realm of Satan, the prince of darkness, and has brought me into the light of Your marvelous love—into the light of knowing Your glory. I rejoice that I no longer need to walk in darkness, for I have the light of life.

Judges 5:31; 2 Corinthians 4:6

Father, may I and my fellow believers absorb Your light more fully and depend on Your strength more constantly. More and more may we triumph in Christ and spread abroad the wonderful fragrance of Your indwelling presence.

2 Corinthians 2:14

Especially defeat Satan in the lives of Your children struggling with various temptations—including the following friends and loved ones:

Anointed with Power

*F*ather, I praise You that Christ, whom You anointed with Your Holy Spirit and power, continues to conquer new territory within me, filling me afresh with Your fullness, Your love, Your power.

Acts 10:38

Thank You that Christ is my risen and victorious Lord, and that in Him I've been anointed with Your Spirit to reign in life—to triumph over sin and over the Evil One with his lies and deceptions. How wonderful to know, Father, that right now Your Spirit intermingles with my spirit in a permanent oneness. I look to Him to continually fill me and to keep me under His influence so that His gracious and immeasurable power will be at work in me, overcoming my flesh and the world and the devil.

2 Corinthians 1:21-22; 1 John 2:20

I rejoice that Your Spirit is here to convict me of sin, to protect me from Satan, and to strengthen me with might. Thank You that this anointing I've received from You abides in me and continues to teach me—and the Spirit's teaching is true and not a lie. And through His truth I've been set free—free from the mastery of sin and the snares of Satan, free to reign in the realm of Real Life. I rejoice that the truth counters Satan's lies. It cancels out his subtle deceptions.

1 John 2:27; John 8:32

I'm especially grateful to You for giving me power to be effective in serving You. I praise You that I can serve by Your Spirit's power mightily at work within me, rather than having to depend on my own strength and abilities.

Acts 1:8; Colossians 1:29

I pray for myself and for the many Christians I know, both individually and in various groups, that we'll be enriched through a growing knowledge of You. And may it dawn on us afresh that You have been made rich because we belong to You—we are Your inheritance! Encourage us through Your Word and the enlightening of Your Spirit. Make us more aware of the tremendous power available to us, to assure victory over all the evil powers we encounter.

Ephesians 1:17-19

And, Father, I praise You that this close relationship with You can also knit me together with other believers by strong ties of love. I realize that loving, harmonious unity with other believers is always one of the great needs in our lives as Your children, and we can count on You to accomplish it. I praise You for the great protection this provides against the attacks and deceptions of our Enemy. May I—and those I pray for—increasingly understand and experience the rich fullness and oneness that is ours in Christ.

Colossians 2:1-2

A Song Within

*L*ord, in my heart I can sing a song of triumph, for victory over the Enemy comes not by might nor by power but by Your Spirit. In myself I'm no match for Satan and his demons. But because of Jesus, our Victor, they face impossible odds. They face the One who made the stars and keeps them in their courses—the magnificent One who humbled Himself to die in agony and shame on the cross. What a joy it is to know that through death He broke the power of Satan, our proud and arrogant Enemy. And to think that I share His power, that in Him I, too, can be invincible!

Zechariah 4:6

Thank You that Christ's death and resurrection paved the way for Your Spirit of power to indwell my spirit. Your Spirit has poured out Your love in my heart. He has become in me a spring of water, welling up into everlasting life and flowing out as rivers of living water.

Romans 5:5; John 4:14; 7:37-39

How thankful I am for times of refreshing that come from Your presence. Time and again I can come before You and be renewed. I can let You breathe new life into my inward person day by day as I feast on the abundance of Your house and drink from the rivers of Your delights.

Acts 3:19; 2 Corinthians 4:16; Psalm 36:8

How deeply grateful I am that by Your Spirit I'm alive with Christ's life and righteous with His righteousness! He is my sufficiency for doing the good works You've planned for me. Thank You for the way this removes the strain from my life—for the way it frees me from the stress of striving in my own strength to please You. It lets me enjoy the calm dews of Your presence with me and in me.

2 Corinthians 3:5-6; Ephesians 2:10; Hosea 14:5

Thank You that You accept me by Your grace, Your unmerited favor. Make me quick to recognize and resist Satan's lie that I must earn Your love and favor by serving You. What good news it is that grace has replaced law keeping as the way to gain and enjoy spiritual life—the life of Christ Himself! To think that through my inner union with Him I'm accepted, I'm okay, and I'm in the process of being conformed to His image. All through grace!

Romans 7:6; Ephesians 1:6; Romans 8:29

I will sing to You, Lord, for You have triumphed gloriously! You are my strength and my song. You have put a new song in my mouth, a song of praise. May many hear it and trust in You. I praise You that when we begin to praise, we open the way for You to defeat the Enemy. We can conquer because we trust in You!

Exodus 15:1-2; Psalm 40:3; 2 Chronicles 20:22

Completely New

*T*hank You, Lord Jesus, that You came into the world to demonstrate not only Your love but also Your power. You came to give Your life as a sacrifice so sufficient that it canceled all my sins. I'm so grateful that Your death and resurrection crossed out the whole debt against me in Your Father's account book and He no longer keeps a record of the laws I've broken. How wonderful that You nailed that account book to the cross and closed the account. As far as the east is from the west, so far have You removed my transgressions from me.

Colossians 2:14; Psalm 103:12

Thank You for stripping the demonic rulers and authorities of their power over us—power to accuse and enslave us. And thank You for exposing them as empty and defeated when You triumphed over them through the Cross and the Resurrection. What deliverance and confidence comes through knowing that Satan is defanged and defeated—that You, crucified and now glorified, have dethroned him, breaking the back of his power as the ruler of this world! Now he desperately attempts to maintain a kingdom for himself and to thwart what You seek to do in people's lives. How grateful I am that all my spiritual battles are against an already-beaten and disarmed Enemy! What wonderfully good news for me to believe and use!

Colossians 2:15; Hebrews 2:14-15; John 12:31

I praise You that You not only removed forever my guilt and sins but You sent Your Spirit to make me a completely new person—a new creation—in my inmost being. In Your eyes I've been cleansed and perfected forever. By faith—by simple confidence in Your Word—I can be assured of this and enjoy a clean conscience. Thank You, Lord!

2 Corinthians 5:17; Hebrews 10:14; 9:14

Thank You also for the privilege of encouraging others to believe this good news. Make me bold in sharing these truths, with believers and unbelievers. Give me grace to take advantage of every opportunity You give, large or small. Help me sow seeds and pray for them in ways that will help defeat Satan's purposes and open their hearts in the coming weeks or months or years—or perhaps today.

Colossians 4:5

I count on You, Lord, to cause me to triumph in You and to spread to those around me the fragrance that results from knowing You. Enable me to never be ashamed of You and Your wonderful message of good news. Allow me to help others (both believers and not-yet believers) to respond to Your knock at the door of their hearts, letting You do all the good things You've promised for them, both in this life and the next.

2 Corinthians 2:14; Revelation 3:20

Good and Mighty Shepherd

*Y*ou prepare a table before me in the presence of my enemies; You have anointed my head with oil." Lord Jesus, You are such a Good Shepherd, such a wise and powerful Leader and Protector! I praise You for the amazing truth that You prepare a spiritual banquet for us and that our spiritual enemies have no power to interfere with our feasting.

Psalm 23:5

You will arise and shepherd Your flock "in the strength of the LORD, in the majesty of the name of the LORD." You, Lord Jesus, are our majestic, kingly Shepherd—great to the ends of the earth. You showed Your greatness in open triumph at the Cross and in the Resurrection. And You show it in invisible triumph now, taking ground from Satan and setting his captives free.

Micah 5:4; Colossians 2:15

I know that in this present world our Enemy is a liar and a vicious lion looking for someone to devour. And as the father of lies, he hates the truth and is constantly propagating false ideas and beliefs. His intentions are always evil. Yet how grateful I am that through You, Lord Jesus, the good purposes of our Father in heaven can prevail in the lives of His children. I rejoice that in You we have everything necessary for life and godliness and victory over the Enemy.

1 Peter 5:8; John 8:44; 2 Peter 1:3

Father, I magnify You with thanksgiving for placing in Your Son all the glorious riches of wisdom and knowledge, both divine and human. How grateful I am that all Your fullness lives bodily in Christ, and that we as ordinary, flawed Christians have this fullness in us. What a magnificent Savior and Lord You've given us! So much greater and more powerful than all evil influences—including the world, the flesh in each of us, and the devil with all his helpers.

Colossians 2:3,9-10

Thank You also for Your Spirit who is my Comforter and Counselor, my Helper and Teacher and intimate Companion. And I praise You that Your Son is preparing a place for us in our eternal home so that where He is, we may be also. And there we'll be forever free from all of Satan's evil intentions and influence!

John 14:16,26,1-3

I pray that these truths about You and Your Son and Your Spirit will become more and more real in my life, counteracting Satan's lies and false promises. May the same be true for my friends and loved ones—especially:

The Best Preoccupation

hank You, Father, that I need not get preoccupied with the devil and all his conspiracies, or with all the fearful coalitions of enemy rulers and hosts that he supervises. Enable me instead to be preoccupied with You, my holy God. I honor You as the God of Exodus 15— majestic in holiness, awesome in praiseworthy deeds, the almighty Warrior who shatters the Enemy. "The LORD is a warrior; the LORD is His name."

Exodus 15:11,3

As I think about the intense spiritual battle we're all in, I may often need to let You tell me, "Take heed, be quiet, do not fear, and do not let your heart be faint." But I need not delve into the power of dark authorities, trying to measure how dangerous they are or pinpoint their specific identities. Thank You that You have revealed in Your Word what we need to know about them and their evil schemes.

Isaiah 7:4 RSV; 2 Corinthians 2:11

How good it is to know that the plans and desires of the Enemy will not stand. As we walk with You, all his schemes and proposals against us will be thwarted and turned to our advantage, for You are with us. So I choose not to fear the Enemy but to fear only You, with reverent trust and with hatred of evil. I choose not to be preoccupied with Satan but with You, my all-powerful and all-prevailing God.

Psalm 46:6-9; Isaiah 41:10; 14:24,27

What a joy it is to remember that You've always been victorious and exalted over all the forces in heaven and earth—natural and supernatural, visible and invisible. I praise You that throughout history You have always been behind the scenes, supervising world events—and supervising the spiritual war against Lucifer and all his evil followers, visible and invisible.

Nehemiah 9:6; Isaiah 2:11-12

So I greatly rejoice that You created all spiritual beings, and You remain supreme over them all, including those who are opposed to You. You are infinitely greater than everything we can see as well as everything we can't see, and this includes all satanic rulers and powers, great and small. Satan is accountable to You, as You've shown us in the case of Job. And how I thank You for the countless heavenly authorities who are on Your side—the holy angels who obey Your slightest desire and who are involved with people here on earth as You see fit.

Job 1:7-12; 2:6; Hebrews 1:7,14

Thank You that I'm never at the mercy of Satan, that I need not let him entice me and trap me in sinful ways. Through Your Word and Spirit make me more aware of his schemes and maneuvers. And I hold fast to this truth: by faith I can stand against him and his evil purposes, both in my life and in the lives of others. I may seldom know just what he's trying to do, or how, but You know. And through You, I can stand firm and come away victorious.

Glory and Shadow

*F*ather, help me not to give Satan any advantage or delight by seeking my own glory in people's eyes. Instead let me constantly give glory to You in new ways, keeping You at center stage as I speak of Your perfections and let You manifest Your presence through me.

Cause me to dwell day by day in Your shadow. I long to live my whole life there, with You in the bright foreground in every situation, in every opportunity. When You work through me, may the praise be Yours. May You be in the limelight as I give all the glory to You and remain in Your shadow.

Psalms 86:12; 91:1; Matthew 5:16

Enable me to glorify You as I pass through each situation in my life— each time of blessing or progress, as well as each river I must cross, each desert I must pass through, each season of flood or drought, of pain or pleasure. May my responses honor You, not me. Deliver me from drawing attention to myself either by moaning and complaining or by subtle boasting and trying to impress. Not to me, O Lord, not to me, but to Your name give glory. This prayer is according to Your will, so I can count on You to answer it!

Psalm 115:1; 1 John 5:14-15

O my awesome God, I worship You for Your glory—glory that excels all others—a radiant outshining that makes all other glories fade and ultimately flicker out in oblivion. Thank You that no one has ever been able to rob You of Your glory or share it with You. I shout for joy that Lucifer lost out when he rebelled against Your rule and aspired to steal Your glory and be like the Most High. How he and his legions cringe at the thought of Your glory! How they resent it when we ascribe to You the honor and glory due Your name and refuse to seek glory for ourselves. How the devil hates it when we enthrone You as Lord of our lives and situations and when we learn to ascribe to You the recognition You rightfully deserve.

Isaiah 48:11; Daniel 4:37

I worship You for Your Majesty as the Most High God, exalted far above all. I worship You for Your brilliance that causes people to fall on their faces before You. I praise Your mighty dignity and awesome beauty as King of all. Yours is a splendor not limited to majestic parades but one that rides forth and wins battles. You're the awesome, glorious Champion, the all-powerful Warrior who prevails against Your enemies.

Psalm 86:9; Isaiah 42:13; Psalm 45:3-4

To You be the glory, both now and forever. Amen!

Romans 11:36; Jude 24-25

Overcoming the World

*T*hank You, Lord, that Your desire is not to take us out of the world but to keep us safe from the Evil One, making us strong and pure and holy as You teach us Your words of truth.

John 17:15-17

How grateful I am that I've been crucified to the world, which lies in the grip of the Evil One, and I can boldly stand against worldly desires to indulge, to possess, to impress. I praise You that though I'm in the world, I'm no longer of the world. Fill me today with a deeper love for You, and make me quickly aware when love for the world creeps in.

1 John 2:16-17; Galatians 2:20; 6:14

Thank You again for redeeming me from indwelling sin—from sin in the flesh—from the patterns and energies of my former way of life. I've been born out of the old life into a new life as a new person in Christ. I rejoice that You've united me with Christ—with His crucifixion, His resurrection, His ascension. What a joy to be assured that Christ *is* my Life—that my life is "hidden with Christ in God" and that I have the Holy Spirit within me to enlighten, to empower, to be my Ally and Mentor and Guide, and to bring a harvest of godly qualities.

2 Corinthians 5:17; Colossians 3:3-4; Galatians 5:22-23

I look forward to the day when my body will be resurrected and sin in my flesh will be left behind, never again to influence me. Thank You that in my innermost being, in my spirit, this separation has already occurred—and that the Cross and the empty tomb stand between my new life and those old patterns and energies.

Romans 6:3-4

I embrace Your promise that by the Spirit I can be free from the downward pull of the flesh. May I throughout this day see myself as You see me; may I count myself dead to sin—separated from it—and alive to You. Make me quickly aware when I let the old ways invade my experience. Enable me by the Holy Spirit to put to death the deeds of the flesh—to make definite, decisive choices against sin and for obedience.

Romans 6:11; 8:13

I praise You that the Holy Spirit is within me to fill me and perform His wonderful ministry in and through me. I yield myself to His loving control and pray that He will produce in me the fruit of the Spirit, to Your glory.

2 Corinthians 7:1; Galatians 5:16

My Unassailable Wall

L ord, I praise You that I can rely on You to protect me—to guard me day and night from the tactics and power of Satan and his evil spirits. I thank You that I can be strong and let my heart take courage, along with all who hope in You.

Psalm 31:24

How I rejoice in Your lovingkindness! I thank You that in any trial I face You see my affliction and know the troubles of my soul, and You don't give me over into the hand of the Enemy. You set my feet in a large place, where I can stand firm and not slip and fall. How good it is to be Your servant and loved one!

Psalm 31:7-8

You are my perfect Refuge, though the worst may come upon me— distress, grief, slander, even persecution. I'm so glad You're my Deliverer when Satan conspires against me, directly or through people, seeking to destroy me emotionally, spiritually, even physically. I take my stand against him in Jesus's name. I trust in You, for You are my God; my times are in Your hand, not in the hand of any enemy, visible or invisible. My destiny is under Your control, not Satan's. I count on You to deliver me in both current and future attacks. My eyes are continually toward You, for You will pluck my feet out of the net.

Psalms 31:14-16; 25:15

I praise You for how You're able to turn my enemies back, to drive them away like chaff before the wind, to pursue them and make their way dark and slippery. I don't need to fret because of the Enemy and his devices, his snares, his attacks, his hindrances and obstacles. In You I can rest and be still and wait patiently for You to work, without fretting or despairing.

Psalms 35:4-6; 37:7

Thank You that as I trust You with a steadfast mind, Your presence is around me as a strong, unassailable wall and beneath me as an everlasting Rock. I rejoice that You're like a wall of fire around me to keep the Enemy away and to provide me with warmth and light. I count on You to keep that wall of protection around me, a wall that Satan cannot penetrate. May Your mighty presence guard my mind and emotions. My life is precious to You; rescue it from the lions.

Isaiah 26:1-4; Zechariah 2:5; Psalm 35:17 NIV

I pray this also for others near and far who are experiencing the Enemy's attacks. I intercede especially for:

My Complete Armor

*T*hank You, Father, for Your gracious and loving command to be strong in You and in Your mighty power, putting on Your full armor. Give me grace to do this day by day, hour by hour.

Ephesians 6:10-11

You tell us that we wrestle not against flesh and blood—against visible enemies—but against the invisible forces of evil—the satanic forces that often work through humans, moving them to resist You and oppose us as Your servants. I affirm with confidence that You are infinitely greater than all these opponents. And I praise You for providing this complete armor so that I can stand firm against my spiritual enemies. I rejoice that I can be assured of victory and protected from every attack the Enemy could ever conceive against me.

Ephesians 6:12-13

Thank You for each piece of armor—the belt of truth...the breastplate of righteousness...the footwear, which the good news of peace supplies...the shield of faith...the helmet of salvation...and the sword of the Spirit, which is Your Word. How I thank You for these, for they are not luxuries or nice options but necessities. They prepare me for righteous living as well as for success in battle. Teach me to wear my armor constantly.

Ephesians 6:14-17

I thank and praise You for the tremendous realities these pieces of armor represent. They're a part of "every spiritual blessing in the heavenlies" that You've lavished on me in Christ. And they're a vital part of Your plan for delivering me from the corrupt and destructive behaviors and thoughts that Satan promotes.

Ephesians 1:3 MLB margin

I praise You that You Yourself are my protective armor, both within me and around me. You're the defense of my life, and I can leave everything quietly to You. "Rock, rescue, refuge, You are all to me. Never shall I be overthrown.... My safety and my honor rest on You."

Psalms 27:1; 62:1-2,7 Moffatt personalized

I thank You, Father, that putting on my armor is so closely linked with putting on the Lord Jesus Christ, for He is the Truth; He is our Righteousness and our Peace; He is the Author of our faith and our salvation; and He is the Word of God. I rejoice that wearing the armor means knowing and experiencing Him in ways that uniquely prepare us for protection and victory.

John 14:6; 1 Corinthians 1:30; Ephesians 2:14; Hebrews 12:2; 2:10; Revelation 19:13

I count on these truths, Lord, as I face the needs and responsibilities of today and the coming days. Bring blessings out of the needs and problems that Satan would like to use as hindrances. And may the same be true for:

Belt of Truth

hank You for the strong belt of truth You ask me to put on as my first piece of armor. How I rejoice in Your revealed truth, which is so powerful, so vital. It serves like a soldier's belt did in ancient times, holding up his flowing garments, letting him move fully and freely without tripping. May the truths of Your Word do the same for me! I rejoice that I can count on You to bring to mind the truth I need in each temptation that comes my way, in each spiritual battle I face.

Ephesians 6:14

Thank You for letting me know that Satan is the Father of Lies and has been a liar from the beginning. I'm so grateful that You have lifted me out of the quicksand of his lies about who You are, about who I am, and about what life is meant to be. Thank You especially for exposing his lies about Your goodness—about Your positive plans and intentions for me, Your plans for my well-being and my highest good. He wants me to believe that You hem me in and hold me back from really living. He wants to lure me into something that looks like Your plan but with subtle and deadly differences. Thank You for how You repeatedly sweep away his lies, big or small, in which I'm tempted to seek refuge or fulfillment.

Jeremiah 29:11

I worship You as the God of truth—good, solid truth. I rejoice that You see and reveal things as they truly are. Your whole Being is reality.

Falseness or falsehood can make no inroads into You. You have no blind spots, no decay through deceit of any kind. All Your words are reliable, never deceiving, never leading astray, never leading to false confidence. You're always faithful, always true to Your promises. You are the Light of my life, and in You there is no darkness at all. So I have no fear of being deceived or defrauded by You, no fear of being let down or forsaken.

Deuteronomy 7:9; Revelation 19:11; 2 Timothy 2:13; 1 John 1:5

I praise You that through Your Word You give me wisdom and understanding so I can experience reality and see things from Your point of view. Thank You, Lord, that as the God of truth, You have ransomed me. And now Your truth keeps me from basing my life on feelings or fantasies. In Your light, I see light.

Colossians 1:9; Psalms 31:5; 36:9

I ask You to implant Your truth in my heart in new ways. Grip my heart day by day with the truths I especially need. As I meditate on Your words, may they deeply penetrate my heart and life so I will not be tripped up or led astray by the world or the flesh or the devil.

Breastplate of Righteousness

*T*hank You, Lord, for calling us to "lay aside the deeds of darkness and put on the armor of light." I'm so glad that our armor isn't some stiff metal covering but is something as beautiful and bright and weightless and flexible as light itself!

Romans 13:12

Thank You especially for the shining breastplate of righteousness that You gave me as I came to trust You as my Savior. What a protection this is for my heart! How grateful I am that You have given me Your righteousness in exchange for my sin—that Your Son, Jesus, actually bore all my sin on the cross, becoming sin for me—and that now I'm righteous in my innermost being. I'm so glad You've made me eternally holy and clean in Your sight, always able to come boldly to Your throne of grace with utter confidence.

Ephesians 6:14; 2 Corinthians 5:21; Hebrews 4:16

I praise You that knowing and believing this helps me live in a way that pleases You, preventing Satan from getting a foothold in my life. I rejoice that in You I have the power to renounce evil and cultivate righteous living. I count on You to lead me today in the paths of righteousness.

Psalm 23:3

I rejoice that the righteousness You've given me is the very righteousness of Christ. What a losing battle it would be if I had to depend

on my own righteousness—on self-righteousness, which is like filthy
rags in Your sight.

1 Corinthians 1:30; Philippians 3:9; Isaiah 64:6

I praise You for being a righteous God. You love righteousness and
hate wickedness. You never have ulterior motives. You're utterly reliable,
and You're always good, never evil. My righteous God, I worship You in
the Spirit, I glory in Christ Jesus, and I choose to put no confidence in
the flesh—in any works of righteousness I myself might be able to produce. I know I have no actual righteousness of my own in Your sight—
and I refuse to try to establish any. Instead, I rest completely in the righteousness that's mine through Your Son—inner righteousness that leads to
righteous living. And thank You for the results of righteousness: peace and
quietness, confidence and gladness now and forever.

Hebrews 1:9; Philippians 3:3; Isaiah 32:17

I'm so grateful for Christ's example in wearing the breastplate: "In right-
eousness He judges and wages war." What a victory word *righteousness* is!
What a power word! "The righteousness of the upright will deliver them."
By faith I accept the liberating truth that my true self is strong and right-
eous through the work of Christ on the cross and through my union with
Him. Therefore I can triumph when the Enemy accuses and attacks.

Revelation 19:11; Proverbs 11:6

Ready with the Gospel of Peace

hank You, Lord, that we can equip our feet with readiness to proclaim the gospel of peace as part of our armor for staying strong in You. How glad I am that it includes a threefold victory over sin —over its penalty, over its power, and eventually over its presence. Thank You for how simple the gospel message is—that Christ died for our sins and was buried and rose again the third day. And thank You for the privilege of sharing this good news simply, with Your Spirit's power and love and sensitivity.

Ephesians 6:15; 3:8 NLT

How I treasure this good news of Christ's victory over sin and Satan— this glad message that tunes us in to the unsearchable riches—the endless treasures—available in Christ. And how grateful I am for the way the gospel protects my feet from wounds that would cause me to fall in battle. Thank You that it sets my heart free to run in the path of Your commands—it turns me from Satan's control to Your gracious rule over me.

Psalm 119:32 NIV

I marvel at how this good news has drawn me into Your kingdom and given me peace with You both now and for all eternity. I'm no

longer Your enemy! I belong to You, along with all who have heard the
gospel and responded with simple faith.

Romans 10:17; 1 Corinthians 1:18

What a joy it is to be at peace with You—to be permanently linked
with You, with all the enmity ended, the alienation gone forever. Thank
You that this "shalom" peace includes wholeness, contentment, harmony,
and well-being. What inner rest this provides—freedom from the turmoil
and anxieties that would drain my strength for battle.

Romans 5:1

But, Lord, how Satan loves to divert us from the gospel of peace and
prod us to fight the wrong battles—fleshly battles with one another as
we step into Your shoes to judge others. The flesh prods us to side with
Satan as the accuser, directing our anger at people. Deliver us from this
temptation!

Romans 14:4

Lord Jesus, You are our deep inner peace even in the midst of battle—
a victorious peace won by the cosmic battle You fought in Gethsemane, on
the cross, and in the resurrection. And because You shepherd us, we can
live in spiritual safety as we let You work in us. Your presence within us
speaks, "Peace, be still," giving a calm sense of protection from the Enemy.

John 16:33; Colossians 1:20; John 14:27

Today I pray for this peace in the lives of Your children—and especially for:

Shield of Faith

*H*ow glad I am, Lord, that the complete armor You've given us includes the shield of faith—a massive shield that prevents damage from the flaming arrows Satan uses to attack our faith and our walk with You.

Ephesians 6:16

Thank You, Lord, that faith comes through feeding on—and counting on—Your Word. And thank You that the shield of faith includes believing everything You've said about Yourself and Your Son and Your Spirit. Thank You for Your grace in which I stand and for all You have provided for me. I count on my position in Christ far above the Enemy and on the indwelling Holy Spirit, who has sealed me and who fills me for obedience and service. I rejoice that I don't have to fight my way to a position of safety. Instead, by simple faith, I choose to resist the Enemy from a platform of safety—safety based on the victory You have already provided. I can reign in life through Christ. I can be strong and stand firm in the faith.

Romans 10:17; 5:2; Ephesians 2:6; 1:13; 5:18; Romans 5:17; 1 Corinthians 16:13

I praise You that I can fix my eyes on Jesus, the Author and Finisher of my faith. I can count on Him as my ever-present Commander and Friend who gives me strength and victory. I choose an attitude of faith and confidence as I face the Enemy in the name and merits of the highest Authority in heaven and on earth—in the name of Jesus, Your Son, the almighty Victor.

Hebrews 12:2

Father, I choose to put on the Lord Jesus Christ as my strength and my shield—my inner and outer protection. In whatever ways Satan desires to defeat me in today's battle, I pray in Jesus's name that You will not let his evil devices succeed. Nullify the Enemy's counsel. Thwart him, upset him, and frustrate his plans. Do not let my Enemy exult over me!

Romans 13:14; Psalm 25:2

Thank You for Your promise that You will be with me, and that You will hide me in the secret shelter of Your presence. So by faith I choose today to dwell in You—to trust in Your all-protective presence, which evil powers cannot pierce. You may let distressing things happen to me, but I count on You to protect me from Satan's purposes. Build a wall around my life, a strong defense grounded on truth after truth that I choose to believe. I thank You that I can live by simple faith, by simple confidence in You and Your all-embracing salvation, past, present, and future. Work deeply in me so that I'll constantly count on the promises You've given, looking to You to work in me, for me, and through me.

Exodus 33:14; Psalms 31:20; 140:13; 56:3

Enable me to use my shield of faith day by day and hour by hour. And do the same for my fellow soldiers—especially:

Helmet of Salvation

*T*hank You, gracious God, for the helmet of salvation—salvation by Jesus's death from the penalty of sin, and salvation by His life in me from the power of sin, from the indwelling fleshly tendencies that can give Satan inroads into my life. "O GOD the Lord, the strength of my salvation, You have covered my head in the day of battle."

Ephesians 6:17; Psalm 140:7

I rejoice that the helmet of salvation protects my thinking and helps assure that You are delivering me from sin and from the snares and attacks of Satan. I realize this doesn't guarantee a trouble-free life, but I thank You that it does guarantee a joyful and purposeful life, no matter what Satan has in mind.

How crafty our Enemy is as he seeks to lead me astray from sincere and pure devotion to You! How deeply he wants to wound and control me. And how easy it is to let the world squeeze me into its mold, into its ways of thinking. Enable me to fully commit my mind to You in all that I think and in all that I expose it to. Give me grace to be careful what I listen to and think about, knowing that my life is shaped by my thoughts. And may I not think of myself more highly than I ought to. May I make no provision for the flesh in my thought life, to satisfy its cravings.

2 Corinthians 11:3; Romans 12:2-3; 13:14

I'm so grateful I can count on You to work in me afresh day by day and hour by hour, saving me from all sin. May my thinking and my loyalties and my plans be centered in You and Your Word, letting You show me how to use my time, where to focus my attention, and how to handle my emotions. Thank You for the way this frees You to do so many of the things I pray for. It lets You remold my mind from within, so I can experience Your good and totally perfect will. It opens the way for me to become more fully pleasing to You. And it helps me resist Satan's determined attempts to manipulate my thinking and words and actions so they fit into his plans. Save me, Lord, from his influence!

Romans 12:2

Thank You for inviting me to live more and more in Your presence, where I refuse to dwell on sin in my mind or set any evil thing before my eyes. Help me, Lord, to fix my mind more constantly on Your Word and on Your incomparable love and beauty and perfections. May my mind and heart be filled with delight in You as the High King of heaven, awesome in holiness, mighty to save. Throughout each day, help me stay focused on things that are true and pure—on things that are lovely and kind and gracious.

Psalm 101:3; Colossians 3:1-2; Philippians 4:8

I pray that You'll enable me to wear my helmet day by day, enjoying Your protection of my mind and my thoughts. And do the same for my fellow soldiers—especially:

Sword of the Spirit

*H*ow gracious a provision You've made, Lord, by giving us the sword of the Holy Spirit—Your written Word which is our weapon for both offense and defense. I rejoice at how it attacks the Enemy and thwarts his purposes.

Ephesians 6:17

Thank You that Your Word pierces like fire and crushes like a sledgehammer. I praise You that Your Word is living and active and sharper than any two-edged sword. It repels Satan and his evil forces, not only in my temptations, but also in my praying and my service. Thank You for using Your Word to give special insights in the midst of battle, insights that advance Your purposes and defeat Satan's schemes. Recalling Your Word injects truth into my mind. It delivers me when Satan tries to distort my thinking and mislead me in how I live and how I relate to You and to people. How I love Your Word!

Jeremiah 23:29; Hebrews 4:12; Psalm 119:97

How thankful I am for the example Jesus gave us when, at each point of attack, He quoted from the Old Testament to defeat Satan's temptings. With joy I recognize that I, too, can quote Your Word aloud, affirming my faith and rebuking evil powers. I rejoice that when I'm tempted, my victories don't depend on my resolutions and good intentions but on Your specific utterances thrust at the Enemy in the power of the Holy Spirit, with an unashamed "It is written."

Matthew 4:4,7,10

Make me quickly aware when our malicious Enemy attacks me by feeding lies into my mind—when he tries to make me question Your goodness or see my present trial or failure as the whole of reality, rather than just one snapshot. Give me grace not to let him sap my strength by going along with his lies and evil intentions. Lead me to fresh scriptures— or to familiar ones—that counter Satan's lies and refocus my heart on Your point of view.

2 Corinthians 2:11

I rejoice that You and Your Word are Truth and that Your truth is powerful when I'm tempted or discouraged or confused and when I fellowship with people or minister to them. What an abundant supply of wisdom and strength I have as I simply believe what You've written and come near to You in prayer and praise! Thank You that Your Word is truth and that You use it to make my life more holy and more useful to You.

Psalm 119:160; John 17:17

I'm so grateful that Your Word has answers to each need and responsibility that concerns me. Help me discover these answers and hide them in my heart. And I pray the same for others I know who are facing temptations or trials:

Speaking with Power

Thank You, Lord, for how You continue in our day to speak with power through Your Word, the sword of the Spirit. You've promised that Your Word will not return to You useless. You send forth Your command over the earth, and Your Word runs swiftly, controlling the forces of nature, defeating the power and schemes of the adversary. Deliver me from letting my experience of Your written-down truth get stale through neglect. Thank You that Your Word is the Bread of Life, which nourishes my soul as I feed on it richly and hide it in my heart—as I let it grip me in a powerful way, just as You intend. May Your Word day by day be the joy and rejoicing of my heart!

Isaiah 55:11; Psalms 147:15; 119:11; Luke 4:4; Jeremiah 15:16 NKJV

I'm grateful for how You use Your Word to speak through us to others, piercing through to people's needs, convicting them of sin, and turning them from darkness to light, from the power of Satan to You. Thank You that the demons tremble when we speak Your Word, as it exposes their lies and shatters their power.

Acts 26:18; James 2:19

I love Your Word especially because it so vividly displays the wonders of who You are: Your heart of love, Your thoughts and values, Your character with its deep concern for me and all people, Your delight in each of Your children, and Your infinite, boundless power to bless Your loved ones and to defeat the purposes of Satan. How grateful I am for this written revelation of who You are and of how I can be a joy to You, fulfilling Your purposes for my life. Your Word reveals what You want for me and from me. It shows how infinitely greater Your power is than our adversary's, as well as how infinitely better Your purposes are than his. How I praise You for this wonderful Book!

Psalm 119:27

I thank You again that Your Word is a sword that cuts through Satan's power and purposes, enabling me to experience You in all I am and in all I do. Use Your Word in my life day by day. Strengthen me through it and tune me in to Your wisdom. Enhance my delight in it and deepen my knowledge of You…increase my trust in You…and enrich my experience of You as I face the needs and demands of daily life. More and more may Your Word be "the joy and rejoicing of my heart; for I am called by Your name, O LORD God of hosts."

Ephesians 6:17; Psalm 1:2; Jeremiah 15:16 NKJV

And I pray that You'll do those same things for my loved ones:

Patterns of Protection

hank You, Almighty God, for the great pattern for protection You've given me in Jesus's prayer in John 17. I pray as He prayed then—that You, dear Father, would preserve and guard me from the Evil One, keeping me safe from Satan's power...that I would live as Your sent one in the world...that I would absorb Your joy more constantly and more fully...that I would be made pure and holy by the truth of Your Word...that I would live in loving unity with other believers...and that I would experience anew Your love, the same mighty love You have for Jesus!

John 17:13,15,17,19,23,26

I praise You that Your Word makes me strong as it lives in me and controls me and that the Holy Spirit enables me to overcome the Evil One as I rely on Him for light and power. I cherish the way Your Spirit makes Your Word alive deep within me in life-changing ways. I rejoice that in every type of circumstance, the truths of Your Word enable me to pray according to Your will and to experience Your answers.

John 15:7; 1 John 2:14; 5:14-15

Thank You for Your warnings not to love the world and its ways. Train me instead to love and serve You the way You want me to. Work in me so that I will continually focus my heart and mind on You and persevere in running the race You've set before me.

1 John 2:15-16; Hebrews 12:1-2

Give me special grace, Lord, not to become entangled in the affairs of this world but to be a good soldier in Your army, willing to endure hardships for You. Show me any ways I fall short in this. Make me alert against the satanic forces that control the world system, as they seek to take me captive through hollow and deceptive ideas. What pressures and temptations come my way from people who don't know You, from many of the world's amusements, and from the Enemy who's at work in them! How glad I am that Your Word and Your Spirit protect me from "empty philosophies and high-sounding nonsense that come from human thinking and from the spiritual powers of this world, rather than from Christ."

2 Timothy 2:3-4; Colossians 2:8 NLT

I'm also grateful that You're a Warrior who does not become weary or tired. You energize me and renew my strength as I wait on You. You give strength both for daily living and for battling against our spiritual Enemy. How grateful I am that when I'm weary and have no strength and stumble badly, I can let You be my strength and vitality.

Isaiah 40:28-31

I pray for renewed strength and vigor for others I know who may be weary:

While Enemies Rage

*Y*ou are at work, Lord, reaching down into the cauldron of this fallen world, drawing people to Yourself and conforming them to Your likeness. And one by one You are bringing many sons and daughters to glory. For all this I praise You. This is Your glorious purpose for humanity's history, and You've been at it all these centuries and millenniums. How wonderful that You let us have a part in fulfilling it!

2 Corinthians 3:18; Hebrews 2:10; Romans 9:22-24

Thank You for letting us know that Satan is shrewd, that he's wise in a perverted way and has thousands of years of experience. Yet not one of the plans he has masterminded against You and Your family and kingdom has truly succeeded. Our Enemy scores many victories in his dark kingdom. He blinds people, plucking away the Word when it is sown. He causes much trouble for believers and for the church, sowing tares, tempting, deceiving—all with Your permission. He may score points in the contest, destroying effectiveness and even taking lives. But he's never able to snatch us out of Your hand.

Genesis 3:1; 2 Corinthians 2:11; 11:3; 11:14; Matthew 13:19,38-39; John 10:29

Thank You that no wisdom, no understanding, no counsel can prevail against You! While kings and peoples of the earth—part of Satan's dominion—rage against You, You sit in the heavens and scoff at them.

Proverbs 21:30-31; Psalm 2:1-4

You are totally in command—the Commander in Chief, the King and Captain of spiritual armies. I praise You, Lord, for You are the Master of breakthroughs against our spiritual enemies. Show Yourself strong today, O God; command strength and victory as You act on our behalf.

2 Samuel 5:20 margin; Psalm 68:28

I honor You because You are infinitely greater than the god of this world, who keeps people in spiritual darkness. You are Light that penetrates into darkened souls, shattering their blindness, opening their eyes. You are Truth that exposes Satan's deceptions and dispels false beliefs and dependencies. You are Spirit that penetrates the spirits of those who believe, giving them eternal life, infusing their innermost being with Your light.

Isaiah 29:18; 2 Corinthians 4:4-6

I praise You that the ultimate victory of our Lord Jesus will extend to all things everywhere, defeating everything evil, both visible and invisible. All evil beings will be banished forever. And there will be no more darkness, for everything will be illumined by Your powerful light. Hallelujah! For our Lord God Almighty reigns!

Revelation 22:3-5; 21:23-25;19:6

The Path to My Destiny

*F*ather, before I received Christ, I was Your enemy. I was on the wrong side in the war between Satan and You. I was born with a fallen nature, born into the wrong kingdom as part of the opposition. And unwittingly, when I knew enough to choose, I repeatedly chose for sin and against You! Unknowingly I signed on with the rebel prince—the god of this world, the prince of the power of the air.

Colossians 1:21; Romans 5:10

How I praise You again for transferring me from that dark domain into the kingdom of Your beloved Son. Through Him You rescued me from the tyrant's power. You opened my eyes so that the truth about Jesus dawned in my heart, causing me to be born again. Now I'm at peace with You—aligned with You, made one with You as a member of Your very own family and a citizen of Your country. You took me from my lowliness and seated me with princes, destined with Christ to inherit the throne of glory. In this world I'm only a stranger, an alien, an exile, a pilgrim heading for my true Homeland, the glorious city You've prepared.

Colossians 1:13; Ephesians 2:19; 1 Samuel 2:8; Psalm 113:5-8; Hebrews 11:13; 13:14

How wonderful that my enmity with You has ended—I'm no longer a "child of wrath," imprisoned in Satan's world system that rightly calls forth Your anger and condemnation. I'm no longer united with sin; I'm no longer condemned. You've made me alive with Christ and able, by

His power, to overcome every trap and attack of our spiritual Enemy. So now I'm fighting on Your side in the ages-long spiritual war. What a relief, what a joy to strive *for* You against the Enemy rather than strive against You!

Ephesians 2:2-6

Yes, You ended my striving against You and my alignment with Your enemies. And at how great a price! You paid for my redemption with the precious blood of Your Son. Once again I gladly praise You for Your abundant love and mercy. Thank You that nothing—even Satan's strongest onslaught—can ever separate me from Your love. Death can't, and life can't. The angels can't, and the demons can't. My fears for today, my worries about tomorrow, and even the powers of hell can't keep Your love away.

Romans 8:38-39

I worship You and count on You to work in me today both to will and to do what pleases You. And may these truths become more real to the new believers in Your family—especially:

The Last Word

*T*hank You, Lord, that You always have the last word, not Satan.

How grateful I am for Your ultimate victory over the devil and all his plans. You will deliver us forever from his presence and all his evil influence, and Your victory will be clearly seen in all the earth. In that day You will fully enforce Satan's defeat, binding him and exiling him to eternal torment. Your kingdom will be exalted above all others, and people from around the world will stream to Your headquarters to hear You teach them Your ways. "Great and marvelous are Your works, Lord God Almighty!... All nations shall come and worship before You."

Revelation 20:10; Micah 4:1-2; Revelation 15:3-4 NKJV

I praise You that You have promised us eternal victory, with total freedom from the presence of sin—and for letting us begin now to share in that victory. I'm so glad that Your salvation brings freedom not only from the penalty of sin but also from the power of sin in our daily lives. Thank You for granting us deliverance from the cravings of indwelling sin and from following its desires and thoughts.

Romans 6:4-7

I eagerly await that day when, by Your personal call to be with You or by Your glorious return, You'll take me to be with You for eternity, along with all believers. Help me focus my heart continually on the wonders of

Your return and Your ultimate, total triumph. I praise You that what we'll then see is far beyond our present imaginings. I look forward to feasting my eyes on Your shining glory, with Your eyes bright like flames of fire and Your face like a brilliant noonday sun. How awesome it will be to hear Your voice thundering like the sound of many waters—like mighty ocean waves and a thousand Niagaras. And how delightful it will be to experience Your warm welcome into Your presence forever. Life's trials will seem so small when we see You!

Revelation 1:12-16

Thank You that when we come fully into Your presence, we'll be like You for eternity, for we'll see You as You really are. I'm so grateful that this is part of the victory You won at the Cross and promised us for the future. How this confident assurance motivates me to live a pure life that glorifies You!

1 Thessalonians 4:16-17; Philippians 3:20-21; 1 John 3:2-3

Behold, You will come quickly, and Your reward will be with You. Even so, come, Lord Jesus!

Revelation 22:7,12,20

More and more may these glorious truths flood my heart with Your strength and power in the midst of life's joys and trials. And I pray the same for:

Encouragement for a Lifetime of Praise

*T*o assure stick-to-it-iveness in your praise adventure, let's take a further look at the importance of praise. God's Word gives still more reasons why praise is more than an obligation, more than a pleasant extra in your walk with God...why it is not optional but essential. If you find yourself lagging in your praise journey, come back to the following pages and let the Lord remotivate you.

Through Praise You Can Strengthen Your Faith

Praise is a basic way both to express our faith and to strengthen it, and strengthened faith is no small benefit. From cover to cover the Bible shows us that faith—or trust—is the basic response God is looking for. Faith moves God to reveal Himself to us and to do His mighty work in us as well as for us. Faith brings victory that changes our circumstances—or victory in the midst of circumstances that don't change.

It's not that praise is a sort of magical incantation that makes us strong in faith and maneuvers God into doing what we want. Rather, through praise we focus on God. We fix our inner eyes on Him with a basic trust in Him. Our praise springs from this simple response of faith, this simple choice to believe God, and praise in turn increases our confidence in Him.

Time after time I've found praise to be a quick route to an assured faith, a faith that rests in God and counts on Him to work. When in one way or another we slip off the freeway of faith, praise is often the ramp that gets us back on.

Not infrequently we slip into distrust because we're frustrated at file folders stuffed with unfinished paperwork—folders that represent unfinished peoplework.

One night we were taking a prayer walk along the beach that borders the Singapore harbor. Suddenly my husband, Warren, remembered an urgent letter he had put off writing. Together we plummeted into laments and regrets, anxious about the problems this might cause the couple waiting for his reply.

After our morbid side trip, we got back to prayer. We praised God that He was sovereign, that He was almighty, and that He had promised to work in answer to prayer. Then Warren asked Him to overrule this delay and praised Him that somehow He would use it for good.

Praise helped us fix our faith on our merciful, all-powerful God who is infinitely greater than our failures. At first we chose to praise with tiny stirrings of faith. Then God freed us from our unbelief and renewed our confidence in Him. Once more praise had been a ramp onto the highway of faith.

The letter was soon on its way. Weeks later we received a reply from our friends, who wrote, "We wouldn't have been ready for your suggestions a week earlier." God had used the delay to get Warren's letter to them at exactly the right time. More reason for praise!

Through praise you can demonstrate your faith in God to work in the present as He has in past centuries. Remember the suffering that Joseph went through: the cruel betrayal by his brothers who sold him into a life of slavery, the agonies of his soul, the false accusations, the years in prison, and the forgetfulness of the butler, which meant two extra years of imprisonment. Yet God allowed all these events for good. He used them to prepare Joseph to be prime minister of the greatest nation on earth.

Through them, He had Joseph in the right place at the right time to keep hundreds of thousands of people alive—including Joseph and his family—during a severe and prolonged famine! How did Joseph evaluate all that had happened? He told his brothers, "You meant evil against me, but God meant it for good" (Genesis 50:20).

Through praise you can follow the example of Paul and Silas in Acts 16. They had been beaten and taken to prison, where their feet were placed in stocks. Talk about pain and discomfort and reasons to postpone praise! Yet in that miserable prison they prayed and sang hymns of praise at about midnight, and suddenly the Lord released them through a special earthquake that hit at exactly the right time, in exactly the right place.

Or you can follow Paul's example when he wrote to the Philippians. This time he was in prison for years. Yet he rejoiced in the Lord, confident that his suffering was accomplishing the deep desire of his heart—the progress of the gospel.

In the twenty-first century, as in the first, praise can increase our faith and release the transforming power of Christ in us and our situations—as well as in people near us or across the globe from us.

Some years ago I read about a woman who began to thank God for her ex-husband and his alcoholism and for all the years of loneliness and heartache she had experienced. As she continued to praise, she became aware of her own self-righteousness and superior attitude toward him and of the way she had been a joyless martyr, immersing herself in self-pity. She confessed her sin, acknowledging that her pride was worse than her husband's alcoholism, and kept on praising and rejoicing.

As time went by, this woman's husband, miles away with no direct influence from her, came to Christ and was delivered from his alcoholism. He returned to her, and they began a new life together. For this woman, praise helped to change both her and her situation.

Even in troubled circumstances, or when God does not choose to work in spectacular ways, praise can help us view our situation through different lenses. It can help produce within us a restful, invigorating inner climate.

And often this change of climate within us helps transform the atmosphere around us, for our new attitudes cause people to react differently to us. We begin to exert a creative and uplifting influence on them.

So praise brings obvious victory, or it enables us to turn apparent defeats (whether dramatic trials or minor irritations) into victory from God's viewpoint. It tunes out the conflicting voices that shatter our faith and block our love, and it tunes us in to God's guidance so that we can discern what action to take, if any.

True praise is unconditional. It helps us accept our situation as it is, whether or not God changes it. Continued praise helps us reach the place where we can say, "Father, I don't want You to remove this problem until You've done all You want to do through it, in me and in others."

THROUGH PRAISE YOU CAN TUNE IN TO GOD'S ENRICHING PRESENCE

Psalm 22:3 tells us that God inhabits the praises of His people. Some versions say He is "enthroned" upon our praises. When we praise, we enthrone God in our lives and circumstances, and He manifests His presence in a special way.

Much as television waves surround us at all times, so God's presence is always in us and with us, though it may not always be evident. Praise can flip the switch that, so to speak, turns on that mighty, glorious presence and tunes us in to His sufficiency. We become filled to overflowing with Him. Our lives become a stage on which He, the leading Actor, reveals Himself in love and power, blessing both us and the people we relate to.

In 1960 my first husband, Dean Denler, was hospitalized in Hong Kong with terminal cancer. At that point praise took on a new importance in Dean's life. He decided that, through praise, he would make his hospital room a special dwelling place for God.

"I'll be praising God for all eternity," he told me, "but only during my brief time on earth can I bring Him joy through praising Him in the midst of pain."

Some months later a close friend was officiating at Dean's funeral. He told those who had gathered, "Dean's room became a sanctuary, his bed a pulpit, and all who came to comfort him were blessed."

Praise did not bring healing of Dean's cancer. But through praise and faith, Dean brought the refreshment of God's presence into a painful situation, honoring God in death as he had in life.

Through Praise You Can Activate God's Power

As you pray and praise the Lord, you can free God to reveal His power as well as His presence. Prayer has been called "the slender nerve that moves the mighty hand of God" (source unknown). Any form of sincere, believing prayer directs God's power into our lives and situations, but this is especially true of prayer blended with praise.

Your praise and thanksgiving can help form a highway—a smooth, level road—on which the Lord can ride forth unhindered to deliver and bless. We see this in Psalm 68:4: "Sing to God, sing praises to His name; lift up a song for Him who rides through the deserts, whose name is the LORD, and exult before Him." And Psalm 50:23 says, "He who sacrifices thank offerings honors me, and he prepares the way so that I may show him the salvation of God" (NIV).

Meditate on the amazing story in 2 Chronicles 20. It's a striking example of what happens when God's people pray with a major emphasis on praise.

The chapter reports a dramatic battle with overwhelming odds against God's people. The main character, King Jehoshaphat, is terrified, so he gathers the people to pray. He begins with praise, extolling God as ruler over all the kingdoms of the earth, so powerful that no one could stand against Him, and the king offers praise for past victories. Then he lays before the Lord his urgent problem: "We are powerless before this great multitude who are coming against us; nor do we know what to do, but our eyes are on You" (v. 12). The reply: "Do not fear or be dismayed…the battle is not yours but God's" (v. 15). And the response: worship and more praise. Notice how King Jehoshaphat sandwiched his simple request for help between two thick slices of praise and worship.

The next day the army went forth to face the enemy, believing and praising God. "And when they began singing and praising" (v. 22), the Lord set ambushes against the enemy forces, and they were totally destroyed. Not one soldier escaped alive.

The result of the battle? Great enrichment. It took three days to gather the treasures found in the enemy camp.

What were the keys that moved God's mighty hand? Much praise, a simple request, faith in God's Word, and then, as a sign of that faith, worship and still more praise. As in an earlier battle during the reign of Jehoshaphat's grandfather, "The sons of Judah conquered because they trusted in the LORD" (2 Chronicles 13:18).

Praise can play a highly significant role in moving the mighty hand of God in your life, bringing not only deliverance but also enrichment for you and glory to His name.

THROUGH PRAISE YOU CAN
PROFIT MORE FROM YOUR TRIALS

Why should you praise and give thanks in the midst of trials? Surely not because all the things that happen to you are in themselves good! The reason for praising in tough situations is found in Romans 8:28: "We know that God causes all things to work together for good to those who love God, to those who are called according to His purpose."

C. H. Welch has elaborated on this truth as follows:

> The Lord may not definitely have planned that this should overtake me, but He has most certainly permitted it. Therefore though it were an attack of an enemy, by the time it reaches me, it has the Lord's permission and therefore all is well. He will make it work together with all life's experiences for good.

Praise can heighten your awareness that distressing circumstances are God's blessings in disguise. Your trials rip away the flimsy fabric of your self-sufficiency. This makes room for God's Spirit to weave into your life a true and solid confidence—the kind of confidence that Paul expressed in Philippians 4:13: "I can do all things through Christ who strengthens me" (NKJV).

As fire melts unrefined silver, bringing the impurities to the surface, so trials bring the "scum" to the top in your life. When you praise God in the midst of a trial, you cooperate with His plan to remove the scum; when you complain, you resist His plan and stir the impurities right back into your character. This means that God, to accomplish His good purposes, may have to send or permit another trial; it may delay the unfolding of His good plan for you and your loved ones.

Through praise you focus your attention on God. You acknowledge Him as your source of overcoming power. You begin to look at your problems from a new perspective—you compare them with your mighty, unlimited God. You see them as molehills rather than mountains, as opportunities rather than hindrances, as steppingstones instead of stumbling blocks. You have a part in making them the prelude to new victories, the raw materials for God's miracles.

Praise helps you obey God's command in James 1:2–4: "When all kinds of trials and temptations crowd into your lives, my brothers, don't resent them as intruders, but welcome them as friends! Realise that they come to test your faith and to produce in you the quality of endurance" (Phillips). Praise is a catalyst that speeds up God's maturing process in your life.

Through Praise You Can Experience Christ as Your Life

In Colossians 3:4 we read, "Christ…is our life." I find this one of the most significant truths in the whole New Testament. The Lord began to open up its meaning to me years ago through a man of God who said, "It's not only true that my life is Christ's, but my life is Christ." What an amazing truth! Christ is my life! And yours! Think of who Christ is and what He is like! Then think of what it means to have Him as your indwelling life—what it means in being obedient and loving, in being adequate, in being joyful. Again and again I enjoy release and strength as I simply say, "Thank You, Father, that Christ is my life."

I find that praise is a tremendous aid in experiencing this truth. Praise stimulates my faith, helping me believe that something tremendous has taken place deep inside me—that God has infused me with the person and life of His Son. As I praise the Lord for who His Son is—pure and holy, loving and powerful—I can go on to praise Him that this is what He is in me.

God has used Romans 6 to greatly expand my experience of this life-changing truth, and year after year the Holy Spirit deepens my understanding of what Paul is saying. I'm still learning more, but I'd like to share with you how this chapter has helped me.

Do you find Romans 6 somewhat confusing? If so, you're not alone! So have I! My husband, Warren, prayed off and on for nine years about what it meant before the Lord gave him his first delightful breakthrough in understanding this chapter. May the Holy Spirit use the following paragraphs to give you glimpses into what Paul is saying—or to deepen your already rich experience of its truths. It may not be the easiest reading. So before you begin, why not pray that the Holy Spirit will teach you?

Be aware that this chapter does not teach us that being "dead to sin" means that sin no longer affects us, that it no longer appeals to us. It does not tell us to envision ourselves as corpses that, when kicked or stomped upon, won't feel a thing, won't get mad, won't hit back. The chapter tells us that we're dead to sin, but in the next breath—in the same sentence— it tells us that we're alive with the resurrected life of Christ.

We see this in verse 11: "Consider yourselves to be dead to sin, but alive to God in Christ Jesus."

Let's take a look at the context of this verse. Paul has been talking about the kind of persons we are, not through our natural birth, but through our spiritual birth. When we were born of the Holy Spirit, we became one with Christ; we were united to Him.

What does this mean to us? It means that we became partakers of Christ's death and all its benefits; we were acquitted from all our guilt, for we "died to sin." We no longer live under the reign of sin.

But the miracle didn't stop there. Because Christ was raised to new life, we were raised with Him as new persons who had new life. God delivered us out of Satan's kingdom of sin and spiritual death, and He lifted us into Christ's kingdom—into the realm called "newness of life." Here in this kingdom we are alive with the very life of our risen Lord. And because we are alive with His life, we're righteous with His righteousness (2 Corinthians 5:21).

So we have ended our relationship with sin and guilt and death and have entered into an intimate, eternal relationship with God. We can relate to Him in a totally new way. We are dead to sin and alive to God.

But what does it mean to be dead to sin? Death never means being annihilated. It means being separated. So in our innermost being we have been separated from sin; sin is no longer our nature, and we no longer need to let it be our master. According to Romans 7, sin still indwells us; the old sinful patterns and potential are still written in our minds and bodies. But we are to see ourselves in the light of the Cross and the empty tomb. These stand within us as powerful barriers between indwelling sinfulness and the new person we truly are in our innermost being. We're to let them serve as a blockade, separating our new selves from what remains of our old sinful tendencies. The Cross and the empty tomb form an immovable boundary between who we were and who we have become, between our former realm of sin and guilt and death and our new realm of righteousness and life.

So we are dead to sin and alive to God. This is not fantasy. It is fact. It's the way things are in our genuine nature—in our innermost person, indwelt by the Holy Spirit, with Christ as our life.

It's not that sin no longer entices us. Sin fights against the Holy Spirit within us for control of our bodies and our personalities. And sin is cagey. It masquerades as our master who deserves our loyalty. It poses as an essential part of us, pretending to be our true nature, concerned about what is best for us. Then if we yield to its demands or swallow its bait, it either dulls our consciences or plagues us with guilt, whipping us even after we confess to the Lord. In countless ways indwelling sin causes us distress, struggles, and defeats.

But from God's viewpoint, it is not our true, new self who sins but sin that still lives in us (Romans 7:17, 20). Our sins spring from our old sinful tendencies that are no longer our true identity. The real you, the real me, hates sin and is aligned against it. The real you is distressed when sin prevails and longs for your whole personality to be conformed to the image of Christ. The real you is dead to sin and alive to God.

Picture in your mind what will happen when you die physically. Your spirit, your personality, the new and true you, will immediately go to be with Christ (2 Corinthians 5:8). You will leave behind all your sinful tendencies, all your old patterns of living. And when Christ returns,

He will give you a new, imperishable, glorious, powerful, spiritual body, totally free of even the slightest remnant of sin and death (1 Corinthians 15:42–44).

Think of the freedom from sin's guilt and power you will then experience! Imagine the total way you will be dead to sin and alive to God! Then let the truth dawn on you: in your innermost being, as a "new creation" through Christ's life in you, this has already happened to you spiritually! This is not make-believe. God says it is true, so it is true.

God wants us to believe Him. He asks us to consider ourselves to be what we are: dead to sin but alive to God in Christ Jesus. He wants us to count on the fact that we have a new nature, a new identity. We're no longer to identify with our old identity, with our former nature, with who we once were, as though no radical change has taken place deep within us. As Christ is one with the Father in life and power, so we are one with Christ in life and power. Sin is no longer our nature; it is no longer our master. We are new persons, dead to sin and alive to God.

Think of it this way: it's as though in your innermost being you were previously a caterpillar; you entered the cocoon of Christ's death and through His resurrection emerged as a butterfly. Now, bit by bit as you follow Christ, the ways you think, feel, choose, and live are also being liberated and transformed. And you look forward to the day when your slowly dying body, with its weakness and sinful tendencies, will be changed into a glorious, radiant body just like our risen Lord's.

Thanking and praising God for these facts will help you see yourself as God sees you. This is vital, for we live as who we see ourselves to be. These truths don't just make you feel better about yourself. Rather, they lay the groundwork for a life of fuller obedience.

You can simply say, "Thank You, Lord, that I have been crucified with Christ. It is no longer I who live, but Christ is living in me. And the life that I now (this moment) live in my body, I live by faith in Your Son, who loved me, and sacrificed Himself for me (see Galatians 2:20). I yield my entire body to You, as an instrument of righteousness, to do Your will. I praise You that Christ in me is infinitely greater than all the power of sin in me. Thank You that He has set me free from the condemnation of sin, and that His resurrected life is more powerful than the downward pull of sin!"

Praise the Lord often for the massive difference He has made in you through your new birth and the new, eternal, spiritual life that is yours in Christ. Such praise can help you view yourself as a new person and therefore live the new life God has in mind for you.

The Holy Spirit wants to saturate our minds with the truths He has revealed in the Bible, including these truths in Romans 6. As we meditate on them and respond with praise for them, He delivers us from begging God for what He has already given us. He wants us to pray; prayer is basic to His working. But He wants us to pray with understanding and with praise.

How do we often pray? We plead for victory when Christ is in us as our more-than-conquering life. We beg for the Holy Spirit as though He were not already indwelling us, as though He were not yearning for our consent to fill and control us and produce His fruit in our lives. We pray for spiritual and emotional resources as though they were external bonuses. We forget that they are part of our birthright in Christ, for in Him, God has blessed us with every possible spiritual blessing, with everything we need for life and godliness (Ephesians 1:3; 2 Peter 1:3). We cry to the Lord to give us things that we already have because He is in us. He says, "I am the bread of life, the water of life, the light of life; I am the way, I am the truth, I am the resurrection and the life—I am what you need" (John 6:35; 7:37; 8:12; 14:6; 11:25). He wants us to reply, "Thank You, Lord, You are! You are my sufficiency this moment, this hour, this day. I'm counting on Your life in me—Your love and patience, Your gentleness and guidance and power—to meet my needs and overflow to others."

When we praise with thanksgiving, we deepen our experience of Christ in us as our Source. He constantly fills us and replenishes our resources as we give ourselves in loving service to other people.

C. S. Lewis wrote that a car is made to run on gas, and it won't run properly on anything else. Likewise, God made us to run on Himself. He is the fuel our spirits were designed to burn and the food our spirits were designed to feed on. So it's no use trying to find inner release and power and fulfillment apart from God. There is no such thing. And God has given us His life and power through our inner union with Christ Jesus our Lord.

As we turn our attention to Christ, focusing on Him and His sufficiency, how can we help but praise Him that He is our life?

THROUGH PRAISE YOU CAN DEMONSTRATE GOD'S REALITY IN A SECULAR, MATERIALISTIC SOCIETY

What are the prevailing views of our age? Many people view life through the lens of naturalism—the belief that all things can be explained by natural causes and that if there is a supernatural realm, it has no effect on the natural world or on our day-by-day living.

A major offshoot of such thinking is secularism, which is one of the most widely embraced views of life in our day. Secularism means that God and His will have no part in life. The only things that really matter are human and materialistic concerns. So the secular person, being indifferent to God or actually rejecting Him, lives only for this present world and its rewards.

As you praise and pray, you make your circumstances and your life a test tube that demonstrates the existence of a personal God, a God who is present and involved and who controls the natural universe. The fact that He intervenes and overrules in your daily situations and concerns becomes clearer to you. This flushes out false views of life that still cling to your thinking. It also makes God more obvious to people around you.

Praise (and we're talking about praise rooted in God's Word, praise bent on God's glory) can also help deliver you from secular values. It turns your attention to spiritual and eternal values; it directs you away from the pleasure and success mentality of our age, which resists all pain and discomfort and delay. And it keeps you from trying to make God answerable to you for what He does or permits.

Praise can free you from wasting your energies by speculating on just exactly how each circumstance in your life could be part of God's plan. Through praising and thanking God, you put your stamp of approval on His unseen purposes. You do this, not because you can figure out the specific whys or hows, but because you trust His love and wisdom. You endorse Paul's words in Romans 11:33–34: "I stand amazed at the fathomless wealth of God's wisdom and God's knowledge. How could man ever understand his reasons for action, or explain his methods of working?" (Phillips).

THROUGH PRAISE YOU CAN
OVERCOME SATAN AND HIS CRAFTY STRATEGIES

Who would have imagined that modern men and women, even the highly educated, would revolt against the spiritual vacuum produced by modern philosophies and, in their revolt, would turn to spiritism, to the occult, to Satan worship? Satan inspired these philosophies; then as people abandon them, he directs them into even greater spiritual bondage.

Most of us as real believers steer clear of such obvious cooperation with Satan. So what does he do? He seeks to get us preoccupied with him in ways that seem to be strategic to our spiritual warfare. He promotes an excessive interest in himself, in his evil assistants, and in just how he has them organized.

It is important to know our Enemy. The Bible gives us vital data about Satan and his accomplices, and we can learn much from experienced spiritual warriors who base their warfare on the Scriptures. But Satan tries to sidetrack us. He seeks to get us enemy-centered rather than Christ-centered. He prods us to delve into intriguing details about him and his cohorts, details we don't need to know in overcoming him—details that are not revealed in the Bible and that may be mere speculations or even lies from evil spirits. In one way or another, Satan tries to get us fascinated, or even obsessed, with him, with demons, with demonization.

One pastor tells how he and his people became snared into giving demons undue prominence in their services. Demons, he said, began to flock to the meetings; demon after demon had to be cast out of people. After all, evil spirits are like their father, the devil. They are proud; they are flattered by lots of attention; they love the limelight. So this pastor and his people backed off from focusing on demons and majored on praise that lifted the Lord high. And they found that most of their trouble with demonization disappeared.

As someone expressed it, "It's a serious mistake to underestimate the power of Satan; it's a tragedy to overestimate it"—or to be overly occupied with it.

As demon influence and oppression increase, so does the urgency of focusing our attention on Jesus as Victor. Jesus came into Satan's territory and won the victory over Satan at every point of the contest, both in His own life and in delivering people from demons. Finally, by means of the Cross, He stripped the demonic authorities of their powers; He exposed them to be empty and defeated as He triumphed over them (Colossians 2:15). Then through the Resurrection, God demonstrated His incomparable, all-prevailing power—power that is now in us and available to us: "He raised him from the dead and gave him the place of highest honour in Heaven—a place that is infinitely superior to any command, authority, power or control, and which carries with it a name far beyond any name that could ever be used in this world or the world to come" (Ephesians 1:20–21, Phillips). God has placed all things under the feet of our Lord

Jesus Christ—and that includes Satan and every one of the evil beings associated with him.

How does this relate to praise? Praise is a powerful weapon against Satan. Satan hates praise. It reminds him that God is still supreme in spite of all his evil efforts throughout the ages. It rubs in the fact of his inferiority, his limitations.

Any praise thwarts Satan. But to make your praise even more powerful against him, couple it with God's Word, and especially with truths that magnify Jesus as Victor. Include praise for the blood of Christ, the victory won on the cross, and the triumph of His resurrection. Extol your risen Lord and His exalted position. Lift up His name in triumphant faith. Such praise is powerful in defeating Satan and his clever deceptions.

We may or may not know the names of our demonic opponents or their rank; we may or may not be well versed in occult practices or in New Age tactics or in just what Satanists are up to. But through praise we can defeat our Enemy; we can thwart his purposes and advance the purposes of our wonderful Lord.

Some years ago I was helping a young woman named Betty, who had grown up in a family that worshiped idols and constantly sought to appease evil spirits. Every time she went home, she felt intense demonic oppression. So we studied the Word of God about Satan and his ways. But far more, we studied about our Victor and how to overcome the Enemy through the Word, through prayer and praise, through putting on the armor of God. The next time Betty returned home, she fortified herself with the truths she had learned—as well as praise for the Lord Jesus Christ, for His triumph over Satan and all his hordes of evil helpers, and for His victorious power. And God protected her from even the slightest demonic oppression. She returned radiant and rejoicing.

We can apply Psalm 149:6 to our spiritual warfare, as we rejoice in God's triumph over the Enemy: "Let the high praises of God be in their mouth, and a two-edged sword in their hand."

Through Praise You Can
Bring Glory and Pleasure to God

Through praise you give God something no one else in heaven or earth can give: the love and adoration of your heart. He chose you before He created the earth; He designed you as a unique original so you would be a special person unlike any other; He made you for Himself. And He has made plans for an intimate relationship with you throughout all eternity. Such a God is not indifferent to your response to Him. Your praise makes Him glad. Your neglect grieves Him.

Did you know that praise can help you fulfill your destiny, your chief purpose in this life and the next? The Westminster Catechism condenses volumes of scriptural truth when it says, "The chief end of man is to glorify God and to enjoy Him forever."

Through worship, praise, and thanksgiving, you minister directly to God, who seeks for people to worship Him. Here lies the most compelling reason for praise.

God does not enjoy your praise because He's conceited and loves the limelight. He enjoys it because praise is an indispensable part of relating to Him, the Creator and Supreme Ruler who is exalted high above all. God is holy and infinite and all-powerful, and you and I are specks in a vast universe who receive from Him life and breath and all things. So worship, praise, and thanksgiving bring needed realism into our fellowship with Him. They make possible a true, deep, mutually satisfying relationship.

But does God delight in all praise?

Sometimes people try to attach praise onto an indifferent or self-willed life, hoping for an emotional lift or special visible rewards. And sometimes even a disobedient Christian can get into the mood of group worship or experience a high while listening to praise music. After all, pagans worshiping false gods can experience times of ecstasy! But neither the disobedient Christian nor the pagan honors the true and living God. So how can their praise be a joy to God?

Worship is more than an emotional turnon. Worship includes offering ourselves to God to be His servants and to do His will—nothing more, nothing less, nothing else. It means that we radically change our goals. We choose basic life goals that are centered in God: to know Him better, to love Him with all our being, to do His will at any cost, to glorify Him, and to please Him.

A friend of mine who serves Christ as a professional in a restricted country came across a quote from Amy Carmichael: "O Lord Jesus, my Beloved, may I be a joy to Thee." She has made this her major and constant prayer request. Above her desire for marriage (she's single and not too young), above her desire for success, above her desire to see friends and loved ones half a world away, she has chosen this supreme desire: "May I be a joy to Thee." That's worship.

In worship you bow humbly before the Lord, yielding to Him as fully as you know how at this point in your life. Out of such surrender and worship flows the kind of praise that fully honors and glorifies and delights God. Out of them flow not only your set times of praise but also, as the hours roll by, moments of spontaneous praise, silent or spoken as the situation requires. You think of who God is or of something He has done. Then your heart overflows with adoration or gratefulness as Paul's did in 1 Timothy 1:17, when he broke into his train of thought with the words, "Now to the King eternal, immortal, invisible, the only God, be honor and glory forever and ever. Amen."

Or you thank and praise Him although your feelings resist rather than assist you. It's all right if your praise comes out of a life that has struggles, a life that still falls short of the glory of God, a life that has defeats that require confession, and a life that slides into emotional low periods. This is part of being human in a fallen world, waiting for the magnificent future God has planned for us—for life on a new earth in a body glorious beyond our wildest imaginings.

It may be that often your praise is joyful and enthusiastic. But God doesn't enjoy your praise on the basis of how warm and happy you're feeling. As C. S. Lewis said, we may honor God more in our low times than in our peak times. You may bring Him special joy when you find yourself depressed or wiped out emotionally—when you look around at a world from which God seems to have vanished, and you choose to trust Him and praise Him in spite of how you feel.

Your worship and praise enrich all that God wants to do through your life. A. W. Tozer wrote, "We're here to be worshipers first and workers only second.... The work done by a worshiper will have eternity in it."

As you fill your life with praise, God will reveal Himself to you in new ways—and not only to you but also through you to other people. More and more, in every situation, you'll shed abroad His fragrance.

What is our chief goal? "To glorify God and to enjoy Him forever," to use the wording of the Westminster Catechism. This is our high calling, our destiny. And praise is one of the greatest, most important ways to fulfill it.

AREN'T YOU GRATEFUL?

Aren't you grateful for the delight and privilege of praising our wonderful God, the most beautiful and generous and trustworthy of all beings?

As the Lord directs your heart to further aspects of who He is and what He does, you may want to begin creating your own paragraphs of praise. You can glean ideas from the Scriptures and from other sources, such as sermons, songs, quotations, and poems.

> By him therefore let us offer the sacrifice of praise to God continually, that is, the fruit of our lips giving thanks to his name. (Hebrews 13:15, KJV)

YOU DON'T JUST BELONG TO CHRIST,

your life is Christ!

Journey with Ruth Myers as she guides you on a healing journey, revealing the Truth and empowering you to make self-acceptance and joy your daily companions. Now you can answer the question "Who are you?" with resounding confidence—and delight in your answer forever.